the creative eye

the creative eye

An artist's guide to
unlocking the
mysteries of
visual perception

HEATHER SPEARS

ARCTURUS

For my son, Daniel Goldenberg

ARCTURUS

Arcturus Publishing Limited
26/27 Bickels Yard
151–153 Bermondsey Street
London SE1 3HA

Published in association with
foulsham
W. Foulsham & Co. Ltd,
The Publishing House, Bennetts Close, Cippenham,
Slough, Berkshire SL1 5AP, England

ISBN: 978-0-572-03315-6

This edition printed in 2007
Copyright © 2007 Arcturus Publishing Limited/Heather Spears

British Library Cataloguing-in-Publication Data: a catalogue
record for this book is available from the British Library

Printed in China

Contents

Introduction

This is a book about drawing – the actual, physical act. And it is written for everyone. Through the many years I have taught people how to draw, I've never wanted to know at the start the different training or abilities of my students – it's been more fun to begin open and empty. Nor have I walked around criticizing, because it bores me – the same mistakes over and over, returning if repressed, with the same frustrations. Better to get it right the first time. In this book I've used the same approach, moving back to the beginnings and prebeginnings where things are usually taken for granted – because what is taken for granted is the key to what follows. This book is full of questions which usually go unasked – and some answers as well.

As you read, you will also be taking time to try out a series of exercises, or experiments. They are designed so you can do them at home: I have imagined you sitting in a room – a room which has become very real as I wrote – doing them as you go along. Some are purely visual; some require some simple drawing tools; they can, of course, also be used in a studio or class. And in one sense they are more than exercises. They are new ways of seeing, which will from now on inform and enrich your art.

Above all *The Creative Eye* is about how and why. You'll be exploring the act of sight – how you see the way you do – and what lies behind seeing; your visual brain. It's tremendously exciting to find out what is actually happening when we look at something, and when we attempt to draw what we see.

It is also useful. This book is a guide to the sources of creativity because it tells you in detail about these sources. You will be reading and learning about the brain and what it is up to.

My exploration into visual perception over many decades has been somewhat selfish. I draw obsessively; and as a working artist, questions about how and why I draw have always fascinated me. As a teacher I've been able to learn from my students by including them in certain isolated experiments and seeing what happened. You will be trying these yourself as you work through the book, coming to them without preparation and without example – and you will be experiencing the world as a stranger place than you imagined.

Meanwhile, in the dominion of science, the study of perception (the process of vision) has taken a tremendous leap forward. My reading has led me here and there in the ongoing maze of theories, arguments, facts and wild guesses. For me, it has always been what works (in drawing) that I am after. If a process in the brain explains why we draw in a certain way, or why we have a problem, then I want to work out a way around, or a way in, or a trick, or a persuasion; I am excited, and this excitement is contagious. I try things out and look for a result, and can even sometimes explain it. Everyone wants to know why something goes wrong, and what can be done to correct this.

The Creative Eye contains many quotations. Artists through the ages have spoken, usually rarely and often deeply, about their art. It's usually the summation of the work of a lifetime. Their words inspire and encourage us. Their marvellous secrets, revealed, dovetail into this new scientific knowledge on how we see – it's as if two rivers converged, or two hands joined together. What a time to be learning to draw!

So this book couldn't have been written before, because the science of perception is so new. To apply both – the words of poets and artists and the findings of neuroscience – sheds new light on our creativity, explains our desire and delight in creating art, and also why art is at times so hazardous, difficult and painful. To use both in process, through the careful, hands-on act of drawing, is now within your grasp. What is going on? This book is here to tell you.

Heather Spears, 2007

The Act of Sight

'. . . What is drawing? How does one learn it? It is working through an invisible wall . . . one must undermine the wall and drill through it slowly and patiently, in my opinion.'

Vincent van Gogh

L ook up from this book, and see what is before you. This is your visual field. Take a moment to experience it without choosing to focus on anything in particular. Chances are you are in a lighted room, with various objects in it, the nearest ones appearing larger because they occupy more of the field. You can recognize them by their shapes, their boundaries. You might already be assigning them names even though you are trying not to allow anything predominate.

You can distinguish luminance – varying tones of darks and lights. You know that an object occluding another must be closer to you. Colours correspond to objects or areas – you might find yourself identifying these colours by name as well. If someone is there and moves, maybe way out on the periphery, you are aware of that movement and if it is familiar you hardly register it. You experience space and depth, perhaps by a slight shifting and trembling of boundaries against backgrounds, or by the blurring of more distant objects and the clarity and texture of those nearby.

Are you seeing everything without choosing? You might be wearing glasses, in which case the frames are visible to you as well, or your hair hangs down and covers some of your field of vision. Did you notice this? You may also have 'floaters' in your eyes, little blobs or crescents. These are visible, though you have learned to discount them.

A brief act of looking begins this book. Looking is also its content, and its conclusion as well – it is an exploration of the act of sight, and how your vision affects your art and creativity.

The visual brain

Much is already known about sight. The eye, with its superficial resemblance to the camera, is on the surface and has been studied for centuries. But while the eye is largely passive, the visual brain is not. Lately, with the help of fMRIs (functional magnetic resonance imaging), the further, active process of seeing is being discovered and described. We know, and can now demonstrate, the modularity of vision. This means that different attributes of what's seen (or even imagined) are processed in different, separately located areas, even at different times. And we can locate and isolate specific cells (out of millions) which process extremely specific information (a shade of colour, a particular direction). Yet we do not know exactly how it all works, or how these processes are 'bound' to give us what we all take for granted – the unified experience of sight. All we know is that there is no master recipient in there, no end station.

The visual brain needs exposure, from birth and shortly thereafter, to a lighted world in order to 'learn to see' and we know that everything it needs for this vital learning is in place at birth and ready to be activated. In this sense vision pre-exists within us. We know that human sight is consensual and that it is a complex process, a task in which the array of chaotic information is transformed, worked out, stored away and made understandable.

What has this to do with art and creativity? Pretty much everything.

The visual brain sees, and sometimes loves what it sees and calls it 'beautiful'. Our desire to create and to look at visual images, be they in line, colour or three-dimensional form, is surely grounded in this love.

A definition of line

As an artist, you are working at a kind of interface between two acts – seeing and making. Of these two, it is the act of making which absorbs you most. Creating art is difficult and requires your full attention; as for the act of seeing, it manages very well on its own. Here we are going to tip the balance, and begin by asking some questions about the act of sight and how it relates to the act of making. To do so we will start with something mysteriously related to both acts – line.

> *Take time now to complete a sentence. It's best if you get hold of paper and pen so you can write it down. Think carefully and complete: 'A line is . . .'*
>
> *This is not a trick question. It is perfectly straightforward. Everyone knows what is meant by line – as in linear, as in drawing. If you had to explain the word clearly to a Martian, could you do so?*

It is likely that you went for an easy definition such as 'a series of connected dots' or 'an edge or horizon' or 'the division between two things'. Or a poetic one, actually describing not what a line is, but what a line can *do*.

Here are some definitions people have come up with:

- a boundary around and between forms
- the beginning of everything
- like a word which qualifies objects and emotions
- any mark that moves from one point to another
- the expression of a creative act
- a spasm in the air – a thought that God has thought
- an exploration
- the distance between two points
- the most spontaneous way to retell or relate an experience
- a sharp boundary
- always more or less dependent on feelings
- an expression of energy
- a horizon, the vein of a leaf, the wrinkles of age in a human face telling of a life of emotions, sufferings and joys
- a row of dots that are joined together.

It is interesting to rearrange these definitions into categories. The largest group are *operative descriptors* rather than definitions – they tell what a line does (what it can be used for), hopping elegantly over the problem of directly defining it. 'A line *can* . . .' should really precede these contributions. Lines can, and often do, express, relate, describe, qualify, define space and tell about edges and boundaries. A line can be said to express – through changes in its quality – energy, movement and feelings. It is the *function* of line to express, and line does this very well. But saying what it can *do* has not explained what it *is*.

The Martian, hearing about it only as the ways it can be used (which are pretty well endless), would still not have a handle on it as a *thing* or know what it looked like.

The second category is the far-out or poetic. These metaphorical images attempt to celebrate the magic of line, its strange ambivalent quality that is felt but not understood. Unfortunately, a Martian would be unable to grasp what a line is by being told it was the beginning of everything, a spasm in the air, or the thought of God.

A third category consists of things that a line definitely is not. It is certainly not movement because it does not move. (That it is associated with movement is something else entirely, which we'll be looking into later.) A line, as understood in drawing, is not a horizon, or the veins in a leaf, or the wrinkles on an aged human face. A horizon is a horizon, a vein is a vein, and a wrinkle is a wrinkle. Here again we are exploring line through images – metaphors – calling the one thing (line) something else in order to come closer to understanding its nature. But a line is itself, though it may well be used to tell about these other things. So we have to eliminate these metaphors as of little use to the pragmatic Martian.

In the last category are those descriptions of line which do apply themselves directly to the question, and do their best to answer it straightforwardly.

To go back to the connected dots, you have to admit that there is something, on some level, different between a series of connected dots and a line.

Make a mental image of each, or try them side by side on a piece of paper.

And now comes the interesting bit. A line is not an edge. A line is only a line. 'The distance between two points' won't do either, because you could draw two points on the paper with (obviously) distance between them, thus fulfilling the definition, and there would still be no line. Nor does a line 'move', though it may well serve to express movement. 'The connection between two points, then' – but this is not perfectly helpful either, because an endless line (for example, a circle or any wobbly oblong) has no points to connect. Besides, I could 'connect' two points with my feet or a piece of string; it's just not quite precise enough.

We need to get back to basics. The line we are talking about and want to describe is just a plain *line*. It exists. It is visible. We use the word and everyone understands it. The search for a proper definition is worthwhile because it will teach us about what we are really dealing with, which is more mysterious and complex than we ever dreamed.

If line is something visible, what do we see? I like the word *mark*. A more pompous description of a mark is an *area of uniform pigment or reflectance*. Let's stick with *mark*. A mark can then be narrowed down (it needs to be, because some marks, for example dots, are not lines). To differentiate it from, say, a smudge or a dot, we must define it further – it is relatively long. It's like a ribbon, with its breadth narrower than its length. Some lines are pretty broad, could even be short and broad, but to be lines this relationship of thick to thin would have to hold.

The fun about getting the definition right is that we already have a consensus. We do indeed know exactly what does and doesn't constitute a line. We are working towards what we already know.

A mark with some sort of length (wider than its breadth) could be called *an extended mark*. So there we have it. Or do we? Where does a line exist? Where is it to be found? It is not hanging before us in space; even the image of it in our minds does not do that. If we now include its location, we should have a full definition of line. *On a surface* will do.

> *Line is an extended mark on a surface.*

The surface is not necessarily flat, though most surfaces tend to be. It could be a large egg, or a globe, even the inner side of a bowl. But it has to be there for the extended mark to be made on it. And in this last sentence is the key, the missing word to make our definition complete. *Made*.

> *Line is an extended mark made on a surface.*

The conspiracy of line

Follow this argument closely. Lines do not exist, unless they are *made*; and that means someone makes them. The outside world is not linear, the visual array is not linear. You may well be convinced that it is (remember the definitions about line being an edge, a horizon). But think again. An edge is not a line.

Edges, what we usually call 'lines', have been described in cautious scientific terms as 'abrupt changes in the amount of light reflected from a surface, which correspond to the boundaries of an object' (Wade and Swanston, *Visual*

Perception). This identifies lines used for representing observed contours – certainly their primary function, but not their only one. The authors go on to remark that well-defined transitions between light and dark are rarely observed, and an outline drawing of an object is 'an abstraction that does not correspond readily to the features of the pattern of light projected from the scene'.

Look up from this book and once more check out your visual field. This time look for edges, where one shape or form stops and another begins. Some overlap and the edge is an occlusion, some consist of a sharp change of direction, like the corner of the room or where wall meets ceiling. In each case the edges are clearly visible. But what is visible? Not lines, but indicators of difference – for example the cessation of one area of colour, texture or tone, and the beginningof another. Edges are meeting-places, but the point of contact is not a line. You might argue that the horizon when you gaze out to sea, or the vein of a leaf, or a human hair, is a line. Yet the word (and the experience of) horizon is something else, usually a change in value. A vein, or a hair, is what it is. Line is something especially human, brought into being by us, its makers. It is God's conspiracy.

To accept this fact is a bit disturbing. There is a kind of unease about not being able to trust that what we see is linear. Painters used to handling colour and tone, or sculptors working in three dimensions, have less difficulty than others, and among others I include not just other artists but anyone who has ever used a marking tool – who as a child has scribbled and then drawn, and subsequently learned to write.

A painter and a sculptor can be representative: if they want, they can pretty well represent what they see. There is something straightforward and accessible about working with colour and form. Painters can reproduce areas of colour and tone; sculptors need not worry about creating an illusion of space through foreshortening or simulating dark and light, because statues are in actual space, and the light on them is real. But when artists use line, they cannot represent directly.

The imagined, linear world

Seamus Heaney's *Seeing Things* is a wonderful collection of poems about perception. In 'Markings' he celebrates the imagined, linear world, and the 'marking' of its surfaces – pieces of clothing left by boys to square off an imagined playing field, which then comes into being, even more magically real after darkness. *You also loved*, he continues, *the spade nicking the first straight edge* along a string in the garden, *pale timber battens* marking off the foundation for a house, the *imaginary line* to be ploughed down a grazed field.

> All these things entered you
> As if they were both the door and what came through it.
> They marked the spot, marked time and held it open.
> A mower parted the bronze sea of corn.
> A windlass hauled the centre out of water.
> Two men with a cross-cut kept it swimming
> Into a felled beech backwards and forwards
> So that they seemed to row the steady earth.

Surrendering line

When you draw, say, in life drawing class, you are probably convinced that you are copying what you see. At least you are trying to, and using line works very well to record an accurate detail or contour. What if you decided, reluctantly, to agree there are no lines on or around the model, and you therefore wanted to restrict yourself, somehow, to making a representation without using line? How would you go about it? Suppose you decided to relinquish line in order to somehow get closer to what is really there. If you could surrender line, you would be surrendering a lie. You might discover something true, something you never knew before.

With a bit of soft charcoal, try making a sketch of an object in your visual field. Or just look up and imagine doing so – drawing it without line.

If you paint, you'll have probably used tone, recording changes of value by smudging. If you've sculpted or modelled with clay, you may have opted for copying the mass of solid form in, say, black or grey. Both these methods would represent aspects of what is there without resorting to line.

Whatever you tried, you probably felt extremely frustrated (as if it was like trying to play the violin wearing mittens). Or you found that line did creep in to some extent. You probably decided it's not possible, without line, to adequately represent the details you know you saw.

Yet this is what the camera does. Look closely at a black-and-white photograph in a newspaper and it is composed only of a pattern of dots or pixels. The camera mechanically records what it is pointed at, and this is what it ends up with – a nonlinear representation. Some artists have laboriously made pictures like this, which close up appear grainy and blurred the way a very enlarged photograph would, but which at a distance reveal enormous detail. Actually, you could have drawn that object in your room in this way and got the same result as the camera, given time and extreme pigheadedness.

Organic line

Sculptors usually draw well. Their knowledge of form gets into their drawings. Michelangelo's drawings were often preparatory studies – he drew with the idea of sculpture ever before him. His 'light source' was his own eyes and his lines were like the cuts of a sharp chisel or modelling tool. In his imagination, even as he drew on a surface, he was delving.

This means that to stay closer to the truth, and use some line, you could delve in this way, pretending that you were making incisions in three-dimensional form. Compare this use of line with its predominant task of describing edge. The imaginary incision has a kind of truth. You could call it an *organic line*.

Look up again at the visual field, and locate a detail which could be represented by organic line. Imagine drawing (incising) underneath an object resting on the floor, or choose some interior detail where one edge presses close against another – a wrinkle on your sleeve or the slit between two fingers, a crease on a cushion or a curtain. Do you have an idea of moving into depth? Try actually drawing, if you wish. Use a point. Do not describe boundaries. Draw only the one detail you can delve. Use only the organic or incising line.

This use of line is the least abstract. It is akin to actually working into the surface of clay or metal or wood or stone – almost, it carves; almost, it is not an *extended mark*. It moves mysteriously back and forth across perceptual boundaries. Almost, your use of line in this natural way redeems it back into the tactile art of sculpture, closing in on the true.

Line as tool

Line is a tool, like the musician's instrument, like a Stradivarius, and it's a huge step forward just to acknowledge this and not take it for granted any more. You recognize an artist's line; like handwriting it is individual and personal. Your line is personal forever. Giacometti acknowledged that many kinds of drawing were not his, and lay outside his 'natural possibilities'; he spoke of ways that did not 'correspond with my sensibilities... the tenseness, the gradation of tenseness, or the lack of tenseness of my hand'. You can realize the potential of your own line and at the same time keep its integrity.

As with an instrument, your range and repertoire can be extended with practice. It is still your personal line and always will be.

Relinquishing line, just temporarily, is a way of making you realize its value. Line is an exquisitely tempered tool, and almost limitlessly capable, as the various definitions suggested – of describing the world in shape and contour, of recording what the eye reads as motion, direction, depth, and duration – and, through its quality, of expressing an enormous range, from great energy, tension and power to the most extreme coolness and sensibility.

The divinity of line

As you come to understand the brain's love of line and pleasure in linear play, you might agree that line can also be called a divine gift. To paraphrase Rodin, who said he believed in God 'because God invented modelling', I believe in God because God invented line. If line drawing is the interface of the brain and the world, it is – in words that can only attempt to convey the experience – a way of standing before the face of God. It has that 'in the beginning' quality to it, of being 'in the world, but not of the world'. Tool, translator, artefact, it is inextricably bound into being human. Its nature is human and it is our way of perceiving the universe. It stains and explains, through the mystery of the act of sight, an otherwise incomprehensible chaos.

Line is a special language, a translation and communication of reality perhaps on a level with verbal language, though universal and silent. It may be the language of Martians. After all, we once conned ourselves into seeing lines on Mars.

Line and the brain

The work of processing visual information – the work of sight – is genetically determined. The primary area in the visual brain is mature at birth, and surrounding visual areas only require exposure at the critical period after birth, to catch up. We are born ready to see. It could be said that vision pre-exists within us.

Visual innocence

Artists long for visual innocence, for a way to see clearly, unhindered by the burden of all they have learned. Physiologically, that innocence has to be a myth, when even at birth our visual system is already organized to interpret the world according to its own rules. Emotionally and intuitively, though, we continue to strive for as much clarity as we can lay our hands on. Or lay our eyes on.

Look again into your upswinging visual field as your eyes leave the page. Sit quiet, let it settle, and imagine being a small baby plunked down before this enormous array, wide eyed, taking it all in without judgement and without understanding. Does your experience of the field alter in any way? Be alert to any subtle changes. We will be exploring ways of 'returning to innocence' – even though it cannot really be done, it might be worth a try. Given our usual way of looking, even a small dusting off of the lens ought to be an improvement – an aid to receiving visual nourishment which, as we will see, is the stuff of creativity.

Inside the brain – indifference, fuss and devotion

Let's stay with line a while longer, and use it as an example. Line has been beautifully called [*that*] *geometry of which, in reality, there is no trace* (Kahnweiler).

If we are conducting our lives as if line existed, we can be pretty sure the trickster is the brain. What is going on in there?

To put things simply, information from the eyes proceeds to the *visual cortex* of the brain, a surface area down at the back and extending to each side. From the main or *primary* visual cortex, called V1, different attributes of vision are relayed to different areas. Our interest in line – the processing of forms with shapes, boundaries and directions – is largely concentrated in the area called V3, the *orientation centre.*

In V3 the work of processing shape by its boundaries falls to billions of neurons called *orientation selective cells.* Each one is fastidiously choosy. In the happy terms of neurobiology, it is *fussy about,* or *devoted to,* visual information about a certain orientation – say, verticality – and is *indifferent* to anything else.

These cells are not randomly located, but distributed in exquisite order, stacked in adjacent columns or chimneys whose preferences gradually change across the area. If a visual stimulus conforms to a certain cell's receptive field, that cell will respond – *response* is a vigorous increase in electrical activity, and can be registered by fMRIs – with a transfer of energy between its field and the surround. With an assembly of cells coded for orientation, this energy charge results in the perception of line.

No further processing is necessary. Meanwhile, the other visual centres, in parallel, are responding to different visual attributes (or almost in parallel – motion is a bit late coming in). What is happening in one system is of interest to the others, but it is as though we are inhabited by a crowd of fairly autonomous consciousnesses. There is no control room where everything gets together and is finally interpreted. The unified experience of vision is a mystery.

Bliss

For now, take a moment to imagine and be grateful for the devotion of the orientation selective cells. For their readiness to be excited by what they love. For their work of abstracting chaos into miraculous geometry.

Close this book and give them a treat by gazing at the drawing on the frontispiece (p. 2) – Michelangelo's studies for the Libyan Sibyl for the Sistine Chapel.

One of my students, Dr John Avery, wrote in his definition of line that 'a line drawing is easier to understand than a photograph (just as music is easier to understand than noise) because part of the work of abstraction has already been done'. Whenever we look at a beautiful drawing, with the brain's hard work already done for us, we experience ease and bliss. Surely too, our desire to create images in line, and our joy in doing so, comes directly from this inner, physiological source. Whenever we draw in line, we flood these precise, thirsty little cells with the purest of water from the clearest spring. Their pleasure is our pleasure. Every little child with a crayon makes lines.

Line's repertoire

How do you usually use line? You have already tried using line in a sculptural way, working as if on a three-dimensional surface, 'making incisions' with your chalk or pencil. But the commonest use of line, which seems too obvious to bother putting into words, is to describe edges. Contour, the bounding line, is the most ordinary use of line in art. In using line this way you are replicating what the brain does.

Contour

In *Inner Vision*, neurobiologist Semir Zeki compares the

work of the artist to the work of the brain: artists use line 'because of the neurophysiology of the visual cortex, where cells that are selectively responsive to… specific orientation predominate'. He notes a 'compelling relationship to the neurophysiology of the organ most critical for producing (art), namely the brain'.

Take the opportunity now to play with another organic line. 'Draw' in imagination, using your finger. Your subject is your other arm and hand. Pull up your sleeve and rest your elbow on your knee, your hand hanging loosely from the wrist. Place your drawing finger on an edge (or contour) of your arm, and from there, follow the long contour forward into the hand, moving your eyes and finger at the same pace. When the contour is occluded by another form, stop. You are not following a silhouette, but touching each continuous edge continuously, then finding another one. Choose the next contour, perhaps one emerging from the one that disappeared, and exactly place your finger. Then again look and touch, your eyes moving in synch with your finger. Proceed slowly in the same direction, out towards and along each of the fingers.

If you have a pencil and sketchbook handy, try this: draw in the same way. Again choose a contour of your arm, and this time place your pencil on your paper. Then look up. Imagine that you are doing what you did before, touching along that edge (this time with a pencil, as if you drew along it) while following it closely with your gaze. Look down only to begin a new contour, and look up again before you begin to draw. Move as before, forward into the fingers. Make as many contours, short or long, as you can see.

Touching with line

The line that imagines it touches the edge of what it sees, just like the delving or *incising* line, nudges that much closer to what is there, and can convey that much more information to the observer and therefore provide more delight. You might argue that these *organic* lines are still ruled by the brain's penchant for abstraction – as they are not copies of what is really there, how can they be called 'more real'? But your *experience* in making them was real, and if you look at them you will find they are almost always more beautiful than the lines you usually draw. More attention opens your vision to more information. Information from the visible world nourishes your sight and your creativity.

Drift

The fixed eye is not fixed. Gradually, unconsciously, the gaze drifts downward, is corrected, and drifts again. Drift is necessary. Eyes which are fixed mechanically, as an experiment, go dark within three seconds. In conscious *fixation* – staring fixedly at one point – the eye is continuously in motion, continuously drifting off course and correcting itself. And in fixation, the duration of the drift is prolonged – drift can consume up to 97 per cent of the time, with only 3 per cent left for corrections. The speed of drift has also been measured. Our eyes can sometimes 'follow' a moving object, for example, a bird or a passing car, across a stationary background, locking in and tracking it to some extent against the stormy visual 'slippage' – the scene let loose and sliding across the retina.

This smooth pursuit is called *nystagmus*. And it has been possible, experimentally, to plot the eye's smooth pursuit of an object set to move across the visual field at about the speed of the drift.

When your eyes, with your touch or pencil, had rounded the hill of the wrist, and began the first descent, did you experience pleasure? It is possible to be sensitive to the drift, and to draw with it. Next time you have the chance to draw a standing model, try keeping your eyes on the model in sympathetic alignment with your moving hand, and see if you can enter the drift – draw the long downward contours as sight and touch walk together, and experience a nice somatic satisfaction.

Line and movement

When we explore the phenomenon of line, the word *movement* invariably turns up. Many people will declare that a line 'moves', without even thinking about it. Line and movement are like close comrades; we intuitively associate the one with the other.

Does line move? Of course not, yet it can produce a very strong idea of movement. Part of this is owing to the physical movement which went into making it. Children often chatter away as they draw, as if they were – and they are – travelling here and there with their line. In this basic sense line is inextricably bound up with movement and temporality – it began in one location and progressed to another (or returned, or whatever), and therefore partook in the passing of time as well. For some reason, the idea of motion and temporality continue to stick to the completed line, and the observer sees something lively, a kind of movement in what is static and unchanging.

Movement and the camera

There are plenty of 'frozen' images around, photographs in which a very fast movement has been caught. Oddly enough these images do not contain that illusory idea of movement conjured up by line. This is why carefully copying photographs of fast movement does not work, and results in drawings, paintings and sculptures which appear frozen or static. Of particular interest is the fleeting expression caught on camera, which often cannot be read. Facial expression is dependent on movement.

Movement and the brain

The way the eyes trace movement has been studied exhaustively by visual psychologists, and now fMRIs can report back on what is going on in the brain.

The centre for movement in the visual cortex is called V5. It is remarkably well organized, and virtually autonomous. Most motion selective cells are also selective to direction – in other words, a cell which is devoted to a certain movement going one way will be indifferent to it as it moves back.

They are all completely indifferent to colour. (It's probably no coincidence that the overwhelming majority of line drawings are monochromatic.) Motion cells are not particular about the kind of motion or whether it makes sense – they do enjoy moving dots, and are said to become extremely excited by unpredictable, random movement like ripples or flames. Though these two examples don't seem to me unpredictable, even if they are forever changing, but inextricably organic. Our pleasure in them is like our pleasure in seeing trees, or fractals. Incoherent movement is something else and may well give motion selective cells a big charge. If you have ever watched a cat or dog in its frenzied attempts to catch a darting laser spot, you can imagine something of what goes on in your head.

A peculiarity of the motion centre is that it's a bit slow to kick in. The brain is said to 'misbind' motion in time – and in the temporal hierarchy of attributes, motion is the one that comes limping in last, by a measurable 70–80 microseconds. A second is a very, very long time in neurological terms. No one knows how the brain manages to conceal this embarrassing fact, but it does, and we experience whatever we see 'at the same time', movement, colour and all.

Blind seeing

Another interesting finding (if not quite so interesting, as we have been led to believe) is that there seems to be a direct path from the retina to the motion centre, bypassing the primary visual cortex. There is another, more primitive, visual system located subcortically, in the area of the brain called the superior colliculus. In the optic tract, a passage branches off to this area; called the optic tectum, it is the equivalent, and only, visual processor in reptiles. If V1 is out of commission you really are blind. Yet people report being able to see fast motion, and its direction. Well, not exactly see it. Detect it – well, hardly that either. They are able to answer questions about it correctly with quite-a-bit-better-than-chance scores. This has been called 'blind seeing'. The research suggests vision may be active without its being consciously experienced.

Is consciousness an extravagance?

It seems that consciousness is not so sacrosanct, so important to sensation and necessary to function as we'd like to believe. Incredibly, the brain can process and act on sensations well before there is time for our conscious registering of them, yet lets us refer back to the event, and allows us the delusion of immediate participation and choice.

Movement and line

The camera can capture a fragment of movement. What then do we see, when we observe movement? It is not a fragment. We perceive instead the *progressive play* of movement.

Is there movement in your visual field? If not, create some by moving your hand slowly and continuously to and fro. Follow the movement with your eyes.

Flow

In a beautiful drawing, the line is often said to *flow*. The word conjures up an image of grace, control, perhaps curve, and certainly movement. As you watched your hand move, this flow was visible, not as a surface detail of this or that part, but imbedded in the movement itself. Seeing movement is seeing the flow rather than the thing flowing, the movement rather than the figure (or tree or whatever) which is in movement. Think of the two words 'in movement'. The very language we use explains it.

*Again watch your hand in movement, and this time
consciously fix your attention on the movement rather
than the object. How could this movement be drawn?*

*Now, as you move your hand, think of trying to watch a
sliver of the movement, say as the hand reaches one end of
its trajectory and is turning back again. You will find that
memory and anticipation make seeing this easier and
easier, as you observe the movement over and over again.
Artists who draw fast movement such as dance depend on
repetition to teach them about movement the eye cannot
determine with one fleeting view. Repetition works where
the frozen image does not. If you were to stop your hand to
stare at it, you'd lose the progressive play, the change
which informs it with life.*

In paying attention to one sliver of movement, your eyes are
always aware of a kind of shredding off of images as it passes
by. Can you picture the motion centre as a vast metropolis,
with its columns of cells rising in the smoky dark, and then
imagine a perceived movement coming through like a gust of
rain, passing and calling into wild, brief life each cell along its
path? Adjacent columns would flare and subside as the energy
moved on. In art this shredding off or flaring and subsiding is
expressed by using many lines, and also by not 'finishing off'
the drawing. Messy paintings or drawings give the idea of
movement, unfinished or repeated contours give the idea of
the open, unfinished gesture, or the movement which has
already passed, gone on into another phase. The direction of
the line follows the flow.

Cartoonists have honed the repeated line down to an icon
– horizontal lines from the back of a running figure indicate

speed, curved lines around an object indicate violent shaking. It would be interesting to trace this visual shorthand back in history. It does not occur on Egyptian frescos where even figures walking forward seem to have come to a standstill, immobilized forever.

Movement in the pose

When next you draw the model, even though the pose is a static one, see whether you can use your understanding of *flow*. Most people see the model as a conglomeration of parts, and consider that their task in drawing her (or him – for simplicity's sake I've chosen to refer to the model throughout the book as female) is to fit these parts together. But if you first see the flow of the pose and pay attention to that, the parts will take care of themselves, and you will achieve the illusion of life (of movement). Draw long lines extending from the source of the pose, gradually finding their way unhindered into the extremities which were so hard to 'connect' when looked at separately.

Movement in art

In the 20th century, artists strove to represent motion in many ways. Duchamp's camera-inspired paintings of movement in 1912 were followed by mobiles (Calder) and kinetic art (Tinguely) which actually move – though sculpture has always had the advantage of the observer's being able to move while looking at it, which seems to me to be a simpler solution.

Line however provides that delight in and idea of motion which works best, giving pleasure to the maker and to the observer. Given its origins and its versatility, we can begin to understand why.

Below is a poem I wrote in appreciation of my students'
many accumulated tries at defining it:

a line is
nothing
it is the turning away of a stone, a shoulder
it is the terrified awareness of absence
faltering into consciousness and speaking itself in a
    whisper
it is this hair, hazardous as grass
it is the ground, your feet splay,
black earth fastens into them.
it is the inside of your mouth
or your genitals, the perfect detail of accident
it is the abstract of the world
it is the slow recording
of what happens between my eye
and the skin of your neck
averting and tightening
over aeons
it is the gunshot stammer
of flames in bracken
it is the track of an insect
dragging itself painfully by millimetres
across the surface of the cortex
or a yell of pain –
finished instantly –
silence of it.
scar of it.

The Edge of the Roof

'Be silent, and sit down, for you are drunk, and this is the edge of the roof.'

Jalaludin Rumi

So far you have been making short ventures into the *visual field*. You're used to the term by now; it simply means the area you can see in front of you. If you move, or move your eyes, the field naturally moves as well, though its size stays the same and it will still contain all the information (in terms of light) received by your eyes. You have already done some minimal exploring in the field, paying attention to different aspects – shape, boundaries, direction, motion and depth – in terms of line, the brain and creativity. The visual field is the given – what we as artists have. Now it can serve as a ready-made stage for the work ahead, which is about ways of seeing. Or about kinds of attention – about choosing to see.

Close your eyes, then open them to the visual field. Try a few times – or rather, don't try, but allow. It's easier to experience this mode of seeing by opening your

*eyes, literally, to your full field of vision, so sit
comfortably, and with closed eyes imagine that you are
looking not forward, but back and down, towards the
nape of your neck. This will relax your eye muscles.
Then, as your eyes feel heavy and at ease, slowly open
them – without trying to focus or shift them about – and
let them rest quietly.*

*This is like the first time you looked at the field,
trying not to choose, just letting things happen. The idea
now is to wait even more passively, and allow the field to
be there.*

*As you open your eyes, don't move them about; keep
them in 'neutral', and let them continue to rest and gaze
quietly. Your focus is in the centre of the field. Now,
keeping it there, gradually let yourself become aware of
what else is present in your field of vision – until you are
able to hold the whole field in your awareness.*

Peripheries

After experiencing this kind of seeing, you'll realize that
you can actually see the whole field. By definition you were
seeing it in some way or other, but this time you saw it with
awareness.

*Ask yourself, where does vision cease and
nothing begin?*

*Try raising your hands and gradually moving them
further away from the centre of the field, as you continue
to gaze forward. Eventually it happens – you can't see
them any more. Explore these vanishing places –
overhead, to the sides and (if you poke your head forward*

you will have room for this part) along the bottom of the
field. These are the boundaries of the visual field –
the peripheries.

How large is the field and what does it include? When you
have looked in this way, you will agree that it is large indeed.
If you managed not to let your gaze shift, the field remained
still. You were looking into a large amount of space with things
in it, within a kind of oval or sloppy circle beyond which, in
every direction, there was nothing.

Let your gaze rest

Though this is a simple exercise, it requires some
concentration at the beginning. Most people have trouble
keeping their eyes (and the field) still. The field is your
personal field and it won't stay there like a mural on the wall
while your eyes move about to focus on various parts. If your
eyes swing around, the obedient field swings around too. This
is the first rule of the game: you have to let your gaze rest in
one place.

Something to gaze at

When you do this exercise in a life drawing class, it's fun to
have the model in the centre of the room – and in the centre
of your visual field. She is, after all, what you're there to draw,
so it's natural to rest your eyes on her. At home, you just need
to choose something (for the sake of not having to keep
referring to it boringly as the 'object' I am going to call it, from
here on in, the potted plant).

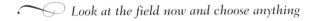 *Look at the field now and choose anything*

you like. It doesn't matter what it is – or even where
it is – because as soon as you focus on it, it automatically
locates itself in the middle of your visual field, which
accommodatingly arranges itself around it.

What you are about to embark on is a kind of adventure –
using your eyes, physically, in a new way.

Whether you decide to draw or not isn't the main issue,
though the drawings, if you make them, will be beautiful and
will be the witnesses to your having seen. The first exercise is
the seeing.

Fix your gaze on the plant (or whatever is your
chosen object), and allow it to rest there. If you want,
close your eyes as you did before and then open them to
rest on the plant. And simply allow yourself, very slowly, to
become aware of the field spreading out in all directions –
and to become aware of the peripheries. Now allow
yourself to explore them just as you did when your hands
were out there appearing and disappearing. But this time
do not use your hands, use your attention. Your gaze is still
resting on the plant. Your attention is on the peripheries,
slowly moving around them until you have completed a
whole circle.

Try this until you are sure you can do it – closing your
eyes, resting them, opening them – at rest, on the plant –
and then, without shifting your gaze, becoming slowly
aware of the whole array, right out to the edges, or
peripheries. How much, and how far out, can you
be mindful of without moving your gaze from its
resting place?

Attention

It's impossible to shift your gaze without also shifting your attention – but you can indeed shift your attention without shifting your gaze. In other words, it's possible simultaneously to look directly at one thing (potted plant) and pay attention to something else (periphery). This is called *external fixation* – your eyes are not directed there, yet your visual attention is engaged in the peripheral part of the field.

Research into what attention is, and how it affects perception, is in its very early stages; almost nothing is known. The chemical and neurological changes it induces in the brain are enormous. People suffering from Tourette's syndrome are free of their otherwise uncontrollable symptoms when their attention is engaged. You as an artist know of those rare times in making art when your attention takes over and you feel as if you've moved into another kind of experience, a kind of freedom. As you read on, you will discover more about that freedom, and how to achieve it.

Covert attention

This kind of looking is called *covert attention*. You can experience the change in your awareness as your covert attention is engaged – in a sense, you are not 'seeing' any more than you ever did; yet, without moving your eyes, you have allowed yourself to receive and process more information, to enhance your vision.

Right now, treat your attention like the cursor on a computer screen. In his prose poem, 'Paravisual Flooding', poet Christopher Dewdney calls covert attention a 'cursor' that can be moved while the eyes are 'staring fixedly'. While you gaze at the plant, the *cursor of your attention* moves out to explore the edges of your visual field.

What does it mean to be attentive to the peripheries in this way? What is out there? You cannot look directly. At one point there is vision (something seen) and beyond it there is not. Is there a uniform blur and fadeout, or a sharpness, or a shimmering? Are some areas of the periphery different from others?

> *Again, go through the stages of this exercise. Remember that you are practising a new method of seeing, and it may take several tries. The elementary rule is not to shift your gaze. If you do 'lose it', simply close and reopen your eyes and begin again.*

Drawing the peripheries

Making drawings of the peripheries verifies this act of attention. The drawings declare: 'This is what I have seen.' Prepare to make some drawings.

You'll need a few simple materials – a board, newsprint and some soft conté. Your field is large so the paper should be large too, at least A3 size. It can be supported across your lap and a chair or stool in front of you. Across, because you have two eyes and your visual field is wider than it is high – 280 degrees horizontally, only 120 degrees vertically. Before you start, write on the top of the paper: ONLY PERIPHERIES.

> *Repeat the exercise, this time with the conté ready in your hand. With your eyes resting continually on the plant (and definitely not looking down at the page), draw*

only the peripheries. When you have followed the cursor of
your attention all around the peripheries of your visual
field, drawing as you go, you can look down.

It is fun to go into this exercise without any images to check
out. This is your visual field, and only you know what you
have seen.

Difficulties

You're probably dissatisfied with this first effort. The
instructions were hard to take seriously. The idea of drawing
peripheries only, in other words *not what you are looking at*,
doesn't make sense. It is normal to be prejudiced in favour of
your focal point, and only gradually, through two or three
trials, to be able comfortably to redirect your attention
outwards across the field.

More seriously, you may be one of the die-hards – even
though you accept that you are not drawing what you are
looking directly at, you can't quite believe you should keep
your gaze resting there and you have to sneak a look at the
sides of the room in order to get the details, reasoning that, if
your head is fixed, your eyes are allowed to wander.

It is also very difficult, at the start, not to be interested
in your *picture*, so you may have kept breaking off
your gaze to see what was happening to the drawing, thus
defeating the purpose of the experiment – which is not the
drawing *per se*, but the experience of a new way of looking
at reality.

Yet drawing without pausing to look at the drawing has
been around for a long, long time. It is not extraordinary; it is
the natural condition of attention. 'What is this drawing?'

Rodin, as an old man, asked. 'Not once... did I shift my eyes from the model. Why? Because I wanted to be sure that nothing evaded my grasp.'

Despite writing ONLY PERIPHERIES on the page, you may have drawn more in the visual field – if not the plant, objects (or people) distributed around the sides of the room well within the peripheries. Any whole object which you can name is not at the periphery. If you've done this according to plan, your paper will be empty except at the edges.

> *Draw again and ask yourself, what's behind that? What's further out? What's the very last bit of visual information I can see? This is where you should be drawing, away out at the very brink where everything disappears.*

The mystic Simone Weil spoke of attention as 'suspending our thought, leaving it detached, empty... as a man on a mountain who, as he looks forward, sees also below him, without actually looking at them, a great many forests and plains'.

Think about this beautiful description of what it's like to be attentive – can your vision be like this?

Do not explain

Many people equate *draw* with *explain*. You might find yourself wanting to explain, make understandable, what you see. If you know there is a window out there on the periphery, or a person, or a lamp, your natural inclination is to explain it in some way – square for the window, cabbage head for the person, line and blob-top for the lamp. Can you draw without interpreting? A square or a circle is an interpretation – it is your false knowledge, not what you saw. What you saw was perhaps a vague, dark blur. If you really saw a head, you weren't far enough out – ask yourself, what is it possible to be aware of even *further out* than that, beyond that head, at the edge of the roof, the place at the very brink of seeing, where everything disappears?

A first drawing which takes note of objects and events inside the field isn't 'wrong' – it can witness your slowly expanding process of becoming aware. It is the record of a tidal flood, carrying your attention like a drift on its surface, as you allow each long wave of attention to reach a little further. Draw as literally as possible what you really see. Try using the word *indicate* rather than the word draw. This may free you from explaining, interpreting, re-creating images from your store of memory or knowledge.

It's possible to trust your eyesight on its own. You may be tempted to resort to familiar swirls and squiggles, reminiscent of Sixties' posters and awful 'visionary' paintings – in a way, it is easier and safer to invent than to choose to look, to revert to what Iris Murdoch called 'the almost irresistible human tendency to seek consolation in fantasy'. I like the word *tentative*, too. A very few, very tentative indications are closer to the truth than a great deal of noisy scrawling.

Again, prepare your paper and write ONLY PERIPHERIES, and begin the exercise by slowly moving into receptive, attentive mode. Don't hurry to be drawing; wait until you are there, eyes calmly at rest on the plant and cursor choosing somewhere on the periphery to begin.

Then indicate what you see out there – right at the brink of sight. Give yourself permission to be scared and tentative, to be empty.

Simone Weil said, 'This way of looking is first of all attention. The soul empties itself of all its own contents in order to receive into itself what it is looking at, just as it is, in all its truth.'

And Rodin said, 'Let us observe, and presuppose nothing. Destiny makes the better choice; do not try to be in the right. Take care rather that the work may be right instead of you.'

Look at the page

Afterwards, look down at the page. You are back in your ordinary, critical, choosy visual mode, and ought to be surprised at what you have made. The page is nearly empty and, at the edges, in a kind of circular arrangement, are these strange markings.

You may see a few wispy lines at the top of the page – a stray strand of hair was hanging down over your forehead. Someone else, with a very weak left eye, records only what the right eye saw, including the 'wall' of one side of her nose. The whole top of someone else's page is black – he has deep-set eyes and heavy brows, and hasn't realized until now that he lives his life as if looking out of a cave. If you wear glasses, something of the rims is visible at or near the peripheries, and recorded. The base of the page might be a mess of rough curves – your moving hand and arm.

These markings may be so light and sparse they can hardly be seen. They may be vigorous and black. Whatever they are

– if you have been able to draw with your attention on the peripheries while gazing at the centre of the field – you are probably looking at the most realistic drawing you ever made in your life.

Entoptic phenomena

You also may have noticed and recorded so-called 'floaters', or *entoptic phenomena* – visible bits and scraps that are actually part of your eye structure. These share the visual field, though we have learned to ignore them.

In *The Flaw*, Robert Lowell plays at the threshold between observer and observed. As you draw in this new way, allow yourself this same questioning, open attitude:

> *Some mote, some eye-flaw, wobbles in the heat,*
> *hair-thin, hair-dark, the fragment of a hair –*
>
> *a noose, a question? All is possible;*
> *if there's free will, it's something like this hair,*
> *inside my eye, outside my eye, yet free,*
> *airless as grace, if the good God... I see.*
> *Our bodies quiver. In this rustling air,*
> *all's possible, all's unpredictable.*

Personal realism

Later we will be looking at the brain's way of interfering with what we see, pushing in with recognition, with stored knowledge, with prejudice and preconception. By drawing something you have never drawn before, you have been able to free yourself to some extent from the brain's interference. That's what I mean by making a realistic drawing.

Everyone's drawings made this way are different. They are true to the vision of the artist who made them – representations of that artist's visual field, no one else's. They are also extraordinarily personal. How can something be realistic and personal at the same time? It can. Your vision is personal, as is your use of your tool – a special handwriting. These drawings are witnesses to the fact that the personal in art takes very good care of itself, and can be left to get on with it.

Christopher Dewdney calls this mode of attention *intelligence*: 'It is as if intelligence was independent of what we normally consider as intelligence, because it operates by stepping out of the way and letting that data arrange itself by its own apparent structure. The height of intelligence is the ability to disappear, to get out of the way.'

Darks and lights, directions, movement

Think of ways to indicate what you see at the edge of sight – to record what lies, visually, outside the range of what you think of as clarity. There is still a kind of clarity, a luminance, but what remains clear out there may be only a slight movement or bit of brightness or tone which, though it can be indicated, need not be made sense of.

Try using the conté laid on its side, indicating areasof darks and lights. Line can indicate direction (the bar of overhead light) and movement (your hand as you draw).

Suprathreshhold luminance

You are making a representation of the edge of nothing. The visual field is an area beyond which, in every direction, there is nothing. Why not just make all the edges black? But no one ever does this, because the nothing out there is not darkness. It is a background of shimmering light, the suprathreshhold luminance. It is the property of vision, yet it seems to give the idea of immense space, what astronomers with the most powerful telescopes have detected out at the far reaches of the universe, a steady echo from the beginnings of time, beyond the most distant galaxies.

 *Make at least two more peripheral drawings.*

The physical response

You are probably really tired by now. And it is an odd sort of tiredness. Some people can't concentrate, and keep having to close their eyes and try again because they've let their gaze slip to the paper. Some feel a kind of wooziness, even nausea. For me there's a warming-up at the outside edges of my eyes and the skin towards each temple feels hot. Photophobia – an adverse reaction to light – is noticed by many. In a room with neon lighting it's especially uncomfortable – 'white noise' you can't help but hate. Or it's no more than heightened sensitivity, of being aware of the reflections on the floor, the glare coming in sideways from a window. Though this may not be on the periphery, it is present in the field as a constant irritation. The plant might have begun to blur, or tremble – some people doing this exercise have noticed a white light forming around the direct object of their gaze.

On the positive side, you may have become conscious of the immense depth, as well as the size, of the field – how far the cursor has to travel, like a spider swinging across a deep background to reach the peripheries. The room becomes like a huge, grey swimming pool – perhaps the way a small child would see it.

Actual, physiological changes occur in your eyes when you use your peripheral vision. The pupils dilate, and this makes things appear slightly fuzzy. This slight loss of sharpness helps you to apprehend the whole without becoming distracted by details.

And when you get back into ordinary seeing mode, something else has happened that isn't ordinary at all – there's a very real intensification of depth vision or *stereopsis*. We will be looking at this aspect of vision later. A few people do not have depth vision, so an intensification of it would not apply to them. For those who have it and never use it – and there are many – the aftermath of this exercise is a revelation.

Get up and move around the room to experience it – or take a walk. You will find that everything stands out in unusual depth and clarity, almost as if furniture, people, trees were cut out of cardboard. A familiar street vista suddenly takes your breath away. This intensity of depth vision will last a while and then gradually fade.

Scale and choice

Pause now to consider what you are learning from these experiments. Using your peripheral vision teaches you to see non-judgementally across the whole field, and acknowledge the relative sizes of items in the visual array – in particular, to appreciate how insignificant a portion of it is taken up by the object in focus. You are learning, by a hands-on method, how we habitually and consistently single out and distort the relative size of items in the field. It is necessary in our daily lives to do so – it is a *compensatory mechanism* that allows us to function – just as we choose what to listen to out of all the noise that continuously assaults our ears. As artists, we must choose and discriminate. But an artist should be aware of choosing, and choose intelligently rather than casually.

The structure of the eye

The eye is a sphere. Light enters the pupil and strikes the retina, the layer of receptors at the back. These cells, like the specialized cells in the cortex, are devoted to certain visual attributes and indifferent to others. The location of each is of prime importance – they form a kind of map of the visual field; it's obvious that a cell would need to be in the direct path of light from a specific part of the field to be activated by it.

Rods and cones

The retinal cells are called *rods* and *cones* because of their shape, and have different functions. The cones are concentrated in the foveal area near the centre. *Fovea* means shallow depression, and it is here, in a little retinal dip, that the main focus of the light is concentrated. Six million cones are densely packed in the fovea. In normal vision, fully 80 per cent of the visual cortex busies itself with information from the fovea, even though the fovea receives input from only 10 per cent of the retinal surface.

Cones respond well to the visible wavelengths of light, many being specialized for wavelengths that we see as colours; yellows nearest the centre, others spread across the retina and blues farthest out. The cones decrease in number the further from the fovea they are located, and there are none at the peripheries.

The rods are much more numerous, numbering 120 million. The further away from the fovea, the more they gain the monopoly, and out towards the peripheries they take over completely.

What were you doing?

When you paid attention to the peripheries, you were activating the rods of your eyes. And if you felt physical discomfort in doing so, there are physical reasons.

Rods are not happy in bright light. They do best with twilight or a dimly lit room, so it is no wonder you felt irritated by the light when you drew. The rods are most comfortable with 'gloom' – twilight, moonlight, half-darkened interiors. Blues and greens, detected further away from the fovea, tend to become more intense in the dusk. Rods are also slower to respond to bright light, and can easily get overloaded – this explains your experience, when drawing in the peripheral mode, of a disturbing pitch of visual 'noise' from the overhead lights, windows or reflections in the floor. Rods are also slowest to recover from a flood of brilliance – we have all noticed how going out into bright light 'bleaches' the world of colour and tone for a short time, and has to be adjusted to. The reverse is true when you set off at night into the woods and have to wait for your eyes 'to get used to the dark'. The rods are able to pick up the mist of steady background luminance. They like being taken for a walk along the river at dusk, when everything is in shades of grey. You may not have noticed the lack of colour as you drew – you were using black and grey on white anyway – but if you think back, you might realize that no, you didn't notice any colour out there. Check it out if you like.

Place a bright-coloured object (say a red shirt) at right angles to a mirror. Stand back so the shirt is in the centre of your visual field and the mirror (with the shirt in it) is at the periphery. Check out the peripheral shirt.

Those who claim to be able to see auras have probably trained themselves to deactivate their focus, and if the long rods of their eyes are particularly well-adapted, perhaps genetically predisposed, the central shimmering created by the unfocused cones can be perceived as colours. In general, this kind of seeing has a 'moral' association – it cannot choose and judge so it is more likely to avoid being clouded or distorted by narrow personal preconceptions and points of view. I find that here, in trying to talk abstractly about ethics, I have used many visual images – *clouded, distorted, narrow, points of view*. Later we will explore what it means (for better and for worse) that vision speaks in words, and words influence vision.

Simone Weil equated attention with prayer (attender means *to wait* in French). She wrote that it is 'a special way of waiting upon truth, setting our hearts upon it, yet not allowing ourselves to go in search of it'.

This is the way you were seeing the world. Physiologically, by removing your attention from the focal point, you were deactivating the cones in the fovea, denying them their customary top dog position. You could not actively *go in search of* the periphery – that would have meant moving your eyes and would not work. So you *set your heart upon it* by paying attention – that *special way of waiting upon truth*.

When attention takes over, the chatter of the mind is stilled. Think back to your experience as you drew the peripheries, how the room became remarkably silent. You can also remember other experiences in your life, and in your art, when you have been able to pay attention. The ability to step aside, to be empty, to disappear, is the essence of creativity.

In Castaneda's *Tales of Power* the sorcerer told the apprentice to walk for hours in the chaparral, gazing before him with his peripheral vision, until the chatter in his mind was stilled. His self-awareness disengaged and he found himself uninterrupted by his consciousness, like a tourist without a camera. This kind of seeing is moral, and ultimately liberating, because it precludes choice: it is to look at the world the way the sun does; it shines on everything – even, as in A. R. Ammon's poem below, on a piece of shit in the dump – with the same brightness.

The City Limits

When you consider the radiance, that it does not withhold itself but pours its abundance without selection into every nook and cranny not overhung or hidden; when you consider

the birds' bones make no awful noise against the light but lie low in the light as in a high testimony; when you consider the radiance, that it will look into the guiltiest

swervings of the weaving heart and bear itself upon them, not flinching into disguise or darkening; when you consider the abundance of such resources as illuminates the glow-blue

bodies and gold-skeined wings of flies arming the dumped

gut of a natural slaughter or the coil of shit and in no way
winces from its storms of generosity; when you consider

that air or vacuum, snow or shale, squid or wolf, rose or
lichen, each is accepted into as much light as it will take,
then the heart moves roomier, the man stands and looks
about, the

leaf does not increase itself above the grass, and the dark
work of the deepest cells is of a tune with May bushes and
fear lit by the breadth of such calmly turns to praise.

This kind of seeing is a pleasure to indulge often. The riverbank at dusk is a good example not only because it pleases the rods in terms of dimness, but also because it allows you to look into water.

When we look at the surface of water in the ordinary way, our knowledge socks in and tells us it is a flat or flattish surface. If you have ever painted water or taken photographs of it, you are already aware of its reflective beauty. Broken reflections endlessly pattern an agitated surface. On a very still day, a lake mirrors its surroundings virtually unchanged. Even a puddle reflects, and reflection gives you messages about depth, messages so convincing that you can see a way in under the far hills, or how the trees stretch upside-down into a puddled street. Next time you look at water, try looking into it instead, using your peripheral vision. Margaret Atwood describes the experience in these lines:

... it's evening and the sidewalk
fills with blue light, you can see down
through it, we walk on water.

Any walk is more extraordinary if you engage peripheral vision. Or as you sit on a bus or train, allow visual flooding, and the passing scene will become a complex, active play of light. You have stopped choosing and separating, and started paying attention to, and enjoying, what is simply there.

Looking at art, making art

I'm convinced this is how Rembrandt saw his landscapes, as well as his peopled compositions; perhaps he saw like this most of the time. Giacometti wrote and spoke about space as if he was constantly aware of it, and of how it was invading and overwhelming him: 'You are disappearing from me. I can't see you any more', he would tell his model despairingly. The quality of visual flooding is apparent in his drawings, in the way he marked the field around the model or whatever he was drawing, just as if he were staking it out – the depth, the peripheries.

Think again, now, of drawing or painting the model (or an apple, or any object you've ever set out to depict). How puny she really is in the great scheme of things – in the expanse of the visual field! A fingernail held near your eye would cover her. What you have learned through these exercises is how constantly you choose, not even realizing you are choosing. The making of choices is central to creativity and should never again be taken lightly. A different choice opens up a new world.

What do you choose to see?

CHAPTER 3

The Thickness of Light
The painter's vision is not a lens,
it trembles to caress the light.

Robert Lowell

T he camera and the eye can both represent the visual
world. They have a basic snapshot similarity, though with
the eye there is already some deformation because of focus
and attention, so the retinal map is not an exact copy as is the
film. The big difference is that the camera is monocular. We
are not. We have two eyes, and they transmit two disparate
images, which are reconstructed into one only inside the
brain. No one knows for sure how this works.

Depth vision

Stereopsis is the experience of depth vision. We have all played
with 3D glasses and devices, and it sounds quite
straightforward. But in actuality very little is known about how
the brain manages to convince us not only that we are seeing
a single image, but also that it can appear three-dimensional.
I say can because the experience of depth vision is not
universal – almost a third of people do not have access to it at

all, and half of those who do have it never use it.

Place a coin on the table in front of you (or draw a small circle). Hold your thumb between your eyes and the coin. Focus on your thumb, moving it forward and back till you find the right distance so two coins appear, one on either side. Now focus on the coin. You should get two thumbs. If this experiment works, you have normal depth vision.

Art and the camera

One-eyed vision gets on quite well, and photographs are useful to artists. But not always. I became interested in the difference when I started drawing babies from photographs. I had always drawn them from life on the neonatal wards, at close hand. Parents would sometimes praise me and say, 'This is the way I see my baby', and I assumed they meant I was accurate. Later, people began sending me photographs of stillborn babies to draw from, and I discovered I could not copy them and get a likeness. (As I usually 'copied' them by eye, it took a while to notice this.) But sometimes with a very difficult face-on head I reverted to tracing the main shapes from an enlarged scan of the photograph. And this carefully and exactly copied drawing looked wrong – quite different, scrawny and narrow. I realized then that I had never been copying exactly. Only by 'intuitively' widening the face, and adding more height to the head, could I make the drawing look like the photograph. Only, it would seem, by making it *unlike*, could I make it *like*. What was going on?

Living likeness

Two things. First, the camera sees with one eye. And because we have two eyes, and hold a baby very close to us, we have to see more. This was what the parents meant when they said I drew the way they saw their baby.

I would imagine a portrait of an adult seated at a distance could be copied perfectly well from a photograph. Yet David Hockney's drawings of adults (in *Secret Knowledge*), made with the optical lens, are sometimes corrected by eye – to show, for example, more of the ears.

Secondly, we have become used to the one-eyed camera and we accept its images as likenesses, even pictures of babies. There is learning involved – adults who have never seen photographs before can't make them out. Over time and repeated exposure the brain recognizes a camera likeness, and accommodates.

But a drawing? It would seem that a linear representation must follow the dictates of the visual system to be acceptable. It is in line and therefore – we seem to demand this – it *must have* been recorded with two eyes, with all the active processing into line which accompanies and completes the act of sight. Armed with our finely tuned ability to read likeness, we look *expecting to recognize* the face we'd see if we were looking at someone directly.

A comment on one sub-species of art-work could be inserted here: portraits 'obviously' made from photographs. Besides the frozen expression (often with rows of teeth) another sign we're picking up could be the slightly pinched faces, especially noticeable in portraits of children made this way. Children, like babies, are mostly seen up close.

Peculiar space

The average viewing distance is 68mm ($2^{1}/_{2}$in) and

convergence occurs most dramatically at about 18cm (7in) – about where you'd hold your baby. Nearby stereoscopic vision is subjective; its space is said to be 'peculiar' in that it does not mimic measured space. There is a distortion: nearby volume is rich and distance is shrunken; familiar objects (your hands, for example) take on a fixed volume even when one is held close and one further away.

Hold out your two hands and move them about. They continue to look the same size, even though the nearer one would have to be covering much more of your visual field – in a photograph, it will of course appear huge. Within this 'peculiar space', the brain is said to 'compensate'.

The two ways of seeing – camera and eyes – are very different indeed. Which is real? Neither, of course. Both are representations. Which is the 'truest' representation? Maybe by now, you've waded through enough about the mystery of sight to say 'Pass' on this one. It is something to think about.

Depth and monocular vision

Using monocular vision, we are still able to navigate in depth and judge distances. There are many clues that teach us about depth without using stereopsis. They are pretty obvious – you can tell where objects are in space by their apparent size, by *foreshortening* (the truncated appearance of forms seen behind one another, as when a model takes a reclining pose with her feet towards your face). *Overlap* or occlusion tells you something is nearer to you than something else, as do shadows. Colours change with distance in predictable ways, and *texture gradient* means how things get progressively more blurred with distance. The biggest clue is *perspective*.

Perspective

Alberti is credited with discovering the laws of linear perspective in 1435. It became the rational substitute for the perception of space, and was utterly convincing. Artists loved it, and chances are that you also spent happy hours, probably in your teens, learning about it and making perspective drawings, fascinated by the illusion of distance you could command. Perspective as a *tour de force* flourished in the Renaissance: a complex building or interior was often included in a painting just so the artist could show off his mastery.

Linear perspective is monocular, deriving from a single, fixed point. The camera with its one eye obeys these same laws automatically, with its fixed point locked in place. Back then, the same effect was achieved by closing one eye. Artists devised grids and drew foreshortened poses through them. Each square was reproduced accurately and the shapes assembled themselves into forms that appeared to be deeply thrust into space. Apprentices went outside to paint landscapes or buildings on sheets of glass, which then became used in the studio the way photographs often are today. Both grid and glass are flat, and whatever was copied through them was seen as flat, and copied mechanically. Optical devices, so painstakingly researched and re-created by David Hockney, were used to cast the image against a canvas or wall. Today, people are being taught to draw freehand in essentially the same way – by discounting or repressing depth vision and considering the world as flat, and copying its various boundaries as if on a grid or sheet of glass.

The first 3D

Sir Charles Wheatstone's surprisingly simple invention of the first 3D device, in 1838, was surprising in that no one had come up with it before, when the way our eyes converge to perceive depth had been generally understood for centuries (even Plato mentioned it).

Imagine a folded greeting card standing so the inside faces away from you, with a small cosmetic mirror glued on each side so you can see into them. Now imagine two pictures, positioned so that one appears in each mirror. The right hand picture is a view as seen with the right eye, the left hand one is the view (slightly different) as seen with the left eye. If you were to tilt in, at a certain distance you would see one picture – in three dimensions.

We don't really see like this

A 3D picture differs in a basic way from how we perceive real depth, in that everything in the picture is in focus at once, with each plane appearing cut out, rather like pieces of cardboard. In reality, we can focus only on one plane at a time – our eyes are said to 'converge' there.

Reread Lowell's lines at the beginning of the chapter (p. 54).

How we see depth, the experience of stereoscopic perspective, is not like monocular, mechanistic perspective, and it is not like a 3D device either. True 'binocular' perspective trembles and shimmers, is never experienced as hard and static. We have already mentioned the quality of edges out there, the quality of the seen as almost ungraspable. We reach out and it changes, slips away from us as if we were trying to catch at water. The drawings of the British artist Stephen Wiltshire have this quality – many are reproduced in *Floating Cities*, drawings he made in Venice and St Petersburg when he was a little boy. Drawn in unlearned binocular perspective, they are both accurate and magical.

Drawing infants close up in the brightly lit incubators, I struggled with what I supposed was my failure to see – I just wasn't good enough at it to record their subtly shaped heads with the exactness I desired. I usually ended up with many tentative lines. On the neonatal ward in Copenhagen, the diagnosis of the baby would be written above the incubator. This poem is about drawing a baby under observation – 'Hydrocephalus obs'. Though I wrote it in ignorance, it somehow manages to describe what was happening with my vision.

I would not have noticed.
All newborn heads
are large, are tender, are strange.
They could be planets, their form
the most difficult abstract in the world.
What is there to see? She is asleep, her hands
curled at her well-formed face.
And now I trace
and retrace the simple profile of that head
from nape to brow, over and over
as if it were changing, its edge
trembling to change, like water swelling towards light.
Even when I get it right, it will not be right.

I now know that my 'inaccuracy' was structured into my vision as I gazed with my two eyes, in depth, my brain convincing me (or doing its best to convince me) that I saw one image, my eyes unconvinced, despairing, trying to grasp what remains ungraspable, what can never be pinned down.

Rivalry

Binocular space, like the idea of the two hemispheres, is a mystery. An elusive, trembly, changing quality imbues everything we see. Visual psychologists call this attribute *rivalry*. What we see has a disturbing, flashing nature – edges seem to flicker and oscillate. Sparkle, lustre, sheen are the products of visual rivalry, the one eye seeing one attribute, the other simultaneously seeing another. Jewels twinkle. All kinds of surfaces and textures owe their beauty to this binocular separation and the brain's ability to recombine and achieve this layered, complex perception.

Gerard Manley Hopkins' poem 'Pied Beauty' celebrates our delight in this aspect of sight. It's central to the pleasure artists take in painting – having fun creating surfaces.

> *Glory be to God for dappled things –*
> *For skies a couple-colour as a brinded cow;*
> *For rose-moles all in stipple upon trout that swim;*
> *Fresh-firecoal chestnut-falls; finches' wings;*
> *Landscape plotted and pieced – fold, fallow and plough;*
> *And all trades, their gear and tackle and trim.*
> *All things counter, original, spare, strange;*
> *Whatever is fickle, freckled (who knows how?)*
> *With swift, slow; sweet, sour; adazzle, dim;*
> *He fathers-forth whose beauty is past change:*
>   *Praise him.*

Binocular rivalry in the research lab means that two dissimilar images, one presented to each eye, can be perceived only one at a time. Our conscious perception of the other view is switched off for seconds, sometimes minutes at a time. It is argued that during binocular rivalry, stereopsis cannot occur because the images travel on different pathways to the brain and competition between the eyes is resolved at a lower level. Do we really stop perceiving? Some visual processes just close down, yet others keep operating when we have no conscious access to them. I can't see how this kind of binocular rivalry can be of direct interest to the artist, but the possibility of alternating on-off switches is curious. You have probably seen visual illusions like the duck-cat or the Necker cube, and experienced how only one view is possible attentionally (there is no way you can 'see' the duck at the same time as you 'see' the cat). Is there a certain wobbly control over how and when you alternate between the images? Vision is indeed filled with mysteries.

How does stereopsis work?

There is still no agreed theory on how depth perception works – how the visual system actually does it, though much research is going on. It is closely linked to the work of deconstructing into line, where information passes through layers of the cortex triggering off orientation cells selective for different angles – the idea of angles seems to hold the key. The cells being studied are called *disparity selective* cells. They are found in V1, activated by stimulus from both eyes, and are repeatedly represented in other areas. Disparity and orientation selective cells are said to overlap to form a topographical map.

Imagine columnar architecture, like skyscrapers – hypercolumns of orientation selective cells rising on a diagonal and, crossing them like orderly clouds or ripples, the disparity selective cells in rows of blobby waves, or wavering blobs, swollen where disparity dominates, squeezed where there is no preference. This tiny, tantalizing image has actually been seen on fMRIs, like a fragment torn from a map of an unknown country.

There is still no agreement about how a map of angles, if this is what it is, can be converted to or perceived as a representation of the world in depth.

Losing and regaining depth vision

We noted the sudden enhancement of depth vision after the peripheral exercises – and for some it might have been the first conscious experience of stereopsis. You may be able to pinpoint other moments when your vision was stepped up a notch, when 'everything came clear'.

I've also experienced the sudden return of stereoscopy after a long period indoors at the computer screen – to go out for a walk brings it back; it feels almost as if trees and other objects come rearing at me to shove me aside. The experience of passing a wall, a person or a tree, of going under or around, up a slope or down one, is extraordinarily tactile.

The neurologist Oliver Sacks writes of his experience of regaining stereoscopy in *A Leg to Stand On*. Recovering from a fracture, he had been moved to a larger room:

'I was settling myself, with delight, when I suddenly noticed something most strange. Everything close to me had its proper solidity, spaciousness, depth – but everything further away was totally flat... I have very good depth perception and I suddenly realized that something had happened to my sense of depth and stereoscopy, that it stopped, quite suddenly, a few feet in front of me – that I was still enclosed, visually, in a transparent box... the precise size of the "cell" I had occupied for twenty days... Depth, stereoscopy, returned in jumps, like the jerky opening-out of a visual concertina, over a period of about two hours; and even then it was not complete... I was amazed and fascinated by these visual experiences... Stereoscopy, so it seemed, had partly disappeared, to precisely the extent of my visual deprivation... I had never realized before that stereoscopy *could* be confined.'

Emotional vision

The capacity for depth vision is measurably altered by attention and mood change. You have probably experienced times in your life when colours seem more brilliant than usual. Happiness, falling in love, any sudden, positive change in mood – a psychological insight or breakthrough (that Aha! moment) brings with it new, if unfortunately short-lived, heightening and clarity of the senses. It is the feeling of being emptied out, freed from the clutter of illusion and projection. We have an idea of being 'able' to receive the visible and audible information which surrounds us. What is happening in the brain? 'Emotional vision' has been recorded on fMRIs. Cells in a visual area called the *amygdala* respond vigorously whenever we are strongly affected by what we see, and depth vision is enhanced.

A stranger accuracy

For the artist, the experience of seeing in depth will always be a mystery, frustrating and rewarding. You want to be accurate, yet not as a camera is accurate. The ability to see deep into space is a stranger accuracy. We need to consider how our special, human, binocular vision can be utilized and celebrated in our art.

Space

Giacometti drew his subjects hundreds of times. He was supremely literal in sticking to his vision and what it revealed to him. Nothing else counted except what he was seeing. James Lord, who sat for him, recorded the process in *A Giacometti Portrait*. Here is what he wrote about Giacometti's space:

'Space is like a heavy, cloudy liquid that is seen no less than the mass... is seen, and is no less tangible. The mass has an energy that is turned in upon self, violently compressed around a central core... The space has an energy that... often seems held back, drawn in by the mass at its centre. Where one meets the other there is an interpenetration. This conception of mass and space as composed of the same substance has a primeval sound, suggesting the creation of stars.'

Try gazing once again towards the potted plant using your peripheral vision. But this time allow your attention to linger on the space close to and touching it. Can you still see the plant as if it were on a stage, located in a certain place on a certain plane? Can you see with depth, see how the plant is immersed or embedded in the space, which both weighs down on it and embraces it? Could you draw that space and how it touches the plant? Make a drawing if you like.

Sur-faces

Try not to see an edge as the edge of a container; see it as a *sur-face* – a passive, external cliff face against which the air (or the floor) presses and flows.

Choose one edge of a solid form (your hand, or another object you can see) and make a careful drawing of the way it meets space.

Envisage, not your familiar hand, but a solid mass against which space breaks and eddies and sometimes finds its way in front of and behind and around. Space is like a 'heavy, cloudy liquid'. Ask yourself exactly how it is stopped – its bays and fjords and rounding promontories. Where does it press sharply, and where does it pour softly across?

Could you draw, for example, a model in this way? Think of the pressure of tons and tons of air and the model as a kind of diving bell, submerged under miles and miles of atmosphere, perfectly adjusted to her aeroquatic, planetary life.

The quality of space, the thickness of light

The Italians used the term *sfumato*, from the word *fumo* (smoke), to describe the vaporous effect, the mellowing and blurring of contours, which came into practice with Raphael and Leonardo and seemed to give life to their pictures by leaving something to the imagination. It was a technique – in that the smoky light of distant vistas was deliberately used to express extremely shallow differences in depth – but it was also the record of a perceptual reality. As you gaze at contours, you find that they are very different from the hard edges you expected. Think too of the Dutch phrase *de dikte der lucht* (the thickness of light) which describes so beautifully what you are becoming aware of.

The most prosaic level

This awareness, despite the imagery, is different from invention and fantasy. It's easier sometimes to fantasize than to pay attention to what you actually see. But you need to stay open and questioning at the most prosaic level. The visual information you receive – the light that is falling on the object in the space it displaces – is not uniform, and there are areas around the object, touching it, that appear sharper and more defined than others. Your depth vision provides a way in. It is this change between sharpness and obscurity that you have to look for, remaining attentive to the space just there, where it touches.

Bays and promontories

The meetings of space and object can be called bays and promontories. If you are really exploring the space, you will find that your drawing will witness to it – it will be much more odd, irregular and craggy than usual.

We'll be exploring later how the brain's knowledge blinds us. When we draw exclusively what we think we know, we invariably regularize it, smoothing out bumps, opening compressions and angles. In drawing, for example, the model, we fail to witness her uniqueness of a particular pose, because we are not paying attention to how she displaces space. If we find out the shape of the space we can get it right.

Meeting places

Peripheral seeing opens the awareness of depth. If you can retain this wide, empty mode, you can use it to find out about the meeting-place of space and mass.

Look with ordinary focus at your hand or an object. Then move into peripheral mode, and check out the changes. Can you see a shimmering at the edges, an interpenetration? How would you draw or paint this?

The word *interface* has been co-opted and forced into a verb by the computer industry, yet in its original substantive meaning it describes very adequately what we are seeing: 'a surface forming a common boundary between two regions, a place of interaction between two different systems or processes.'

Space in front of things

How, without resorting to fantasy, can you draw space that is invisible? By paying attention to the boundaries.

Gaze before you at a concavity. It can be your hand, supine with cupped fingers – the space formed within them. Or some clothing bundled up to form a bowl-shape. It can be the corner of the sofa. (It can even be the whole room, whose walls and ceiling certainly form a concave space; but find or construct a smaller concavity for the purposes of this exercise.) Could you draw that space?

Your attention is on the space and you can go inside it with your gaze and draw the back, the sides, the top, the base, with all the detail you like.

*Using conté, make a drawing of the concavity.
Use a smudge of grey to push right inside, and fill it
accurately as if it were a container brimming with water.*

By choosing to pay attention to the unfamiliar, you are
rewarded with more information, new information.
Your drawing should reflect this by being more accurate
than usual, more beautiful and with a quality of depth, for
having delved.

Creativity and the artist's vision

Rilke, in his *Letters*, told a story about Cézanne. This first
and perhaps greatest of the moderns began to work seriously
in his fortieth year, and did nothing but work for the
remaining thirty years of his life. 'Ill-tempered, distrustful,
jeered at, in despair,' he painted, 'in continual fury, at
variance with every single one of his works, none of which
seemed to attain what he considered the most indispensable
thing, *la réalization*.'

Once, at the table, a visitor mentioned Balzac's short story,
'The Unknown Masterpiece'. This story, 'with incredible
foresight of coming developments', describes how a painter
destroyed himself when he discovered that there are no
contours – only vibrating transitions. On hearing this,
Cézanne 'stands up from the table in spite of Madame
Brémond, who certainly did not appreciate this kind of
irregularity, and, voiceless with agitation, keeps pointing
toward himself and showing himself, himself, himself, painful
as that may have been'.

Vision, in the quite literal sense, is the artist's source. What is out there, seen with the eyes of the artist who strives as Cézanne did to see the truth, yields huge, unexpected gifts and mysteries. We have been exploring the interdependence, through vision, of the artist and the world. We have learned how choice, through attention, can open the sight.

When space takes over

There is a movement, in this kind of seeing, into spaciousness, when space takes over. To deny it, as the artists bent on linear perspective denied it, and as those who now learn to draw by the monocular copying of 'flattened' areas, is to reject an enormous and generous gift. I am not talking here about the popular drawing exercise called 'negative space' in which you are asked to use that deadened, monocular, 'flat' vision associated with grids and glass. Space is not negative, never flat, and once seen can become the dominant aspect of the field.

One of the advantages of seeing flat 'negative space'(I am not denying there are some) is that it gives you access to a great deal of accuracy unavailable if you 'stay inside' the boundaries of the form you are supposed to be drawing. By shifting your attention to the 'outside' you abandon preconceptions about that form's shape which, as we'll see later, actively interfere with your sight. Think now how it would be if you, in your art, could retain this superficial accuracy, and receive, in addition, the power, generosity and reality of depth? You would no longer be 'filling in' a flat area, but delving, gouging, journeying into the depth which you actually experience, with your eyes. How much truer (and stranger) your work would be then!

A Proper Human Goal

'The freedom which is a proper human goal is the freedom from fantasy, which is the realism of compassion... the experience of accurate vision.'

Iris Murdoch, *The Sovereignty of Good*

W hy should you, as an artist, wish to be freed from fantasy? Is not fantasy the source of creativity? To say otherwise sounds provocative, but the quotation above is worth thinking about.

Freedom from fantasy

Iris Murdoch was a philosopher as well as a novelist, and often used the metaphor of art to explore and explain the good. She equates fantasy with illusion and falsehood. What she calls a 'proper human goal' is the truth, to be got at by freeing oneself from illusion. She also uses the term 'realism' – that compassion is realistic. What does that mean? Pretty much the same as Christ meant when he said 'Love thy neighbour as thyself.'

Think about the opening of the sight, about the non-judgemental seeing you have practised in looking at the visual field. Not to choose or to judge, receiving and accepting, are part of accurate vision. In terms of art and creativity, to be true to one's vision – to see accurately – requires this kind of compassion. You know already that it doesn't mean you have to strive to be accurate as the camera is accurate – it means, rather, to strive to use your own vision accurately. You have already experienced that the seen, if you can manage to see it, is far more generous and mysterious that you ever dreamed.

Being an anthropologist

Suppose you were an anthropologist who had decided to study this society – in particular, artists, what they do, and why. Suppose this anthropologist came from a world where there was no word for art. Imagine stepping back and looking at art as extraordinary, at making art as a very strange occupation. This anthropologist's note-taking might list artists as lonely people making things on their own, and as gatherings of people making similar things, as people under instruction or apprenticeship, and as people who display things for other people to look at and/or purchase. Such a study would require visits to studios, workshops, schools, galleries, public arenas. What is common to these people called artists? That they create (bring to being out of nothing) things of no utilitarian value which give pleasure – or other kinds of emotional satisfaction – to others. That the primary reason they make things isn't to give this pleasure, or even to have completed these things, but some drive they have inside them, something called their creativity. What they do gives them pleasure, and other emotions as well. The completion of the thing has its necessary place, as does the response of other people.

Take the artist in the studio – or, to go back to basics, take you at home or wherever you are, reading this book. Were the anthropologist to study you, what would the notes on you say?

Whatever kind of visual art you engage in, your ground rules are that you make it, that you use tools to make it with, and that the results can be seen. Making art takes skill – the skill to see, which you mastered long ago as a baby, and the skill to handle a tool, which you also gained early on by learning to write. Then, to a much lesser degree but important all the same, the skill of mastering your particular craft.

Skill

Drawing presupposes certain constants and a certain community – a broad base of ability we all share. We don't realize how much we quite simply can. Think for a moment how skilled you are. Your training in sight and all it involves is far behind you, in infancy; you can't even remember learning how to see. As you now know, it came naturally, founded on a visual system pre-wired to lead you into the mystery of line – and you took to line like a fish to water. You can clearly see and discriminate between not only the natural world, but what has been created by others in it. When you look at beautiful drawings you instinctively know if they are true – even when you aren't sure how to reach that truth yourself.

And you are skilled manually. You can make marks on a surface wherever you want to, exact to the millimetre. You might not even remember the effort you put in long ago. If you have ever watched a toddler through the stages of gaining control of the crayon, or a little child copying letters, you'll agree it's hard work.

If you want to recall how you yourself had to work at it, try writing a few words with the hand you don't write

73

with – or in mirror-language, or upside down.

Imagine what it would be like if you did not have this dexterity you take for granted. The anthropologist has to think this way – because in other societies there could be adults who had never learned to write, or held a tool which makes marks. It's as though even those who like to call themselves 'beginners' come to the visual arts supremely accomplished. The tools of the various arts may require some learning, but compared to the skills you've arrived with, it is minor indeed. So the anthropologist would consider you very skilled, and, looking around a drawing class, would probably be unable to differentiate between the 'beginners' and the 'professionals'. Everyone functions at a high level.

Your story

As an artist, you have your own routines about beginning and carrying through a project. Think back on your career as a maker, and see whether you can identify with the following story:

As a child you loved to draw, and were happy with what you made. You drew and coloured repetitively, almost obsessively, and got lots of satisfaction out of what you did. Later, you became more demanding of yourself, wanting to master details, to keep the colours inside the lines, to draw recognizable ponies and princesses, or action figures and robots, copying the images available to you. You hit your teens. You might then have given art a break, then come back to it some years later by taking a drawing course or following a How to Draw manual.

This story, this kind of apprenticeship, is common to our culture. Though parents often have their children (willing or unwilling) take music lessons, most children don't get the same encouragement in art training, and if they attend art classes they are expected to 'be creative' rather than to learn skills; in fact, being good at the kind of detailed drawing pre-teens love is considered less worthy than being able to slap colours around as younger children naturally do. This preference (which is very recent and very Eurocentric) is forgivable, but children's art really is fun to look at, more fun than listening to an instrument badly played. You can't really compare the two arts, because the fundamental skill necessary to make pleasurable visual images is mastered by everyone who can see and use a crayon, whereas playing an instrument demands particular skills learned with long practice by only a few.

A lonely road

But it also means that the child nearing ten or twelve who is really interested in making art will walk a lonely road. In Renaissance Italy you might have been apprenticed to a master, but unless your mother or father happens to be an artist and you are given free run of the materials and space, this doesn't happen nowadays. Maybe you had the perseverance to walk that lonely road. Or you saw an exhibition early on and were suddenly and lastingly inspired to be an artist. Maybe you always knew this was what you wanted to be. Maybe you wish you needn't have chosen a career in something else, and want to get back to it, even part time. Maybe making art has always been your joy and you have made sure you spend as much of your time as possible making. So many courses on every level are available for art study that you could pursue your goal to become a full-time artist, or be an apprentice forever. Maybe right now you are considering being an artist for the first time in your life.

The anthropologist, from an objective point of view, sees all this activity as pretty much of a muchness, and makes the kind of notes about it anthropologists make. Looked at with the anthropologist's detachment, what is happening in a life drawing class, to take a familiar example? Here is a group of people with their clothes on, sitting proximate to a naked person, and grasping sheets of white paper and dark marking tools, and exchanging some sort of currency (the naked person is for some reason receiving rather than paying) to spend a set number of hours in an activity that consists of, well, whatever it is, the anthropologist has yet to discover.

Take a few minutes to consider yourself from the anthropologist's point of view, to see yourself objectively, as an artist, and think about what it is like to begin making art. When you begin, do you consider it a beginning? Think of an empty studio or canvas or sheet of paper and concentrate on the emptiness. Imagine yourself with your tools, ready to start. How does it feel?

Being a beginner

You've been absorbing the fact that, at whatever stage in your art career you find yourself, you are highly skilled. Now take an about turn – and become a beginner.

When you begin, do you feel positive or negative, frightened or excited, calm or jittery? What comes up? Like a goalkeeper who touches the posts ritually at the start of every game, most people have ways of easing themselves into their art, some almost by stealth.

What you are doing now is acknowledging, bringing up into

words, the emotions that accompany your beginnings. You are trying to get a picture of what it is like to make art. The more you can learn about your approach the better, because simply making art is not always that straightforward.

Warming-up

In a drawing class there's usually an agreement that the first few drawings are for what is called 'warming-up'. You needn't take them seriously. Like the pianist, you need to flex your fingers and run through some scales and arpeggios before getting down to business. Warming-up is an image – an athlete going through exercises to get the blood flowing and muscles loosened before the race. Working on your own, you may have other beginning rituals and comforts, even if it is just to clutch a cup of coffee as you enter your work area, or to find your favourite chair. If you begin with warming-up, you can forgive yourself for what comes of it; you need not even criticize yourself because it is just a ritual, a way to get going. How much does the body actually need limbering up in order to make art? It's surely more a case of mind, of attitude. Can you feel inside yourself the difference between how you felt about this less-than-serious work and about the 'real' work? Is there a difference and if so, which is the better way to work? There is no 'right' answer to these questions.

Your body is indeed with you and, how you sit or stand, physical things like the locality, the quality of the light, and your tools are all important. Fussing around to get the setting right, or complaining about it, can take some time at the start, before you really start. Do you have a sense of wanting to delay things, settle in before you can pay attention to what you are making? Do you have a sense of being hindered somehow in spite of your efforts and rituals?

You can try this out with a real period of work, if you are going to drawing classes, or with some drawing here and now. Decide on a subject – your own hand is, as ever, always there as a good model – and begin to draw, trying to listen carefully to what is happening to you, around you – how you feel about beginning. Try to pin it down.

Notice, for example, your position – how you are sitting or standing, and whether it feels satisfactory for you, and whether anything changes as you work – your posture, your breathing. Notice whether you are comfortable or uncomfortable, bored, nervous or excited – and any changes there. And notice the act itself – what it's like to be faced with an empty surface and to begin, what it's like to be at it, what it's like to finish (or not finish) what you are making.

Write it down

It's useful to write on the drawing. Scribble down any passing thought or emotion, even the most trivial. From 'It's very nice to be drawing again', or 'I feel quite excited', and other positive, fairly meaningless statements, you can move on to 'I am quite nervous, as I am really a beginner and the overhead lights are a bit noisy', or in a class (resentfully) 'the model moved', or 'there wasn't enough time to finish' – statements which are useful beginnings because they lead to further information, about what that felt like. The idea is to try to give an honest response.

You are becoming aware of how it is for you personally to make art. And there are as many ways as there are artists.

Perhaps your response was, 'I forgot all about how I felt, and my surroundings, I got so interested in drawing.' No one would presume to argue with such a desirable condition. However, during this drawing with specific directions to pay attention to yourself and your surroundings, the odds for losing yourself in your work are very slim. The idea isn't to change but to stay with the hindrances, in a sense to make them work for you by discussing and understanding them.

> *Draw again, keeping yourself intensely aware, writing at least as much as you draw, say between each stroke. What is going on? You can attend to, and write something about:*
>
> - *feelings when you are about to begin*
> - *place (the space, the light, the heat, the kind of air)*
> - *time (how much you allow yourself and if you feel calm or rushed)*
> - *yourself, physically*
> - *your materials*
> - *the progress of your work and comments you make to yourself about it.*
>
> *What you write should answer questions about feeling – basically, do I feel bad or good about this aspect?*

For every artist, each beginning is a new beginning. Giacometti struggled throughout his life with what he called the 'hopeless discrepancy' between concept and realization; he felt that it was necessary to start his entire career every day, as it were, from scratch.

D. H. Lawrence, who painted with great enthusiasm, loved his beginnings. 'To me it is the most exciting moment, when you have a blank canvas and a big brush full of wet colour, and you plunge. It is just like diving into a pond – when you start frantically to swim… like swimming in a buffeting current and being rather frightened.'

The American painter Peter Hasson commented on his beginnings: 'Usually I don't enter with a calm and quiet mind, but with noise, desperation and confusion.'

Max Ernst also likened his work to immersing himself in water: 'A blind swimmer,' he said, 'I have become the amazed lover of what I have seen.'

Rilke spoke of his creative work in these uncompromising terms: 'Always at the commencement of work that first innocence must be re-achieved, you must return to that unsophisticated spot where the angel discovered you when he brought you the first blinding message… If the angel deigns to come, it will be because you have convinced him, not with tears, but with your humble resolve to be always beginning: to be a beginner!'

Towards an image that works

It's useful to find a kind of 'working model' for the act of making art – a way of picturing as vividly as possible how you function as an artist, and your own way of being creative, bringing it into focus and clarity through a series of images. What are you actually doing?

The hemispheres

The popular folk image these days is that of the brain's two hemispheres – the right brain with its ability to process visual information, and the left brain with its ability to analyse it. We can simplify things and say that the right hemisphere 'knows but cannot speak', while the left 'speaks but cannot know'. Any imparting of information (including any book about drawing) describes, systematizes and codifies, as does any assimilation of information – for example, reading this book and working from it.

It's been found that some gifted individuals show less hemispheric specialization. Giftedness in art 'may be the by-product of a brain that has functionally organized itself in a qualitatively different way', writes neurologist Oliver Sacks. Studying the left brain's usurpation of the special visual language of Sign, he discovered that there are no real fixed, 'hardened' or exclusively committed hemispheric functions. The brain is amazingly redundant, essentially plastic, modified as well as 'pruned' by individual experience.

Try to feel your brain. Try to locate your right hemisphere by following messages from your left eye across the optic chasm over to your right hemisphere.

No, you can't. The really irresolvable problem with the hemispheres as an image is that you can't *feel* the brain, let alone feel it crossed over. Erich Harth wrote in *Windows of the Mind*, 'It has no sensation of its own existence. I never see my own brain, it makes no noises like my stomach. I can't feel its functioning like the pulse-beat of my heart, I can't even squeeze it, pinch it, palpate it. It is the most hidden and unobtrusive part of my body.'

At this point the image runs out. The concept of hemispheric function must remain only abstractly interesting – information *about* function rather than an image *of* it.

Excitement
You may have written something about excitement on your drawing, and probably felt some. What exactly is excitement?

In the moment of beginning, it's a nervy, physical sense of anticipation, a feeling you may or may not like. Something is expected – expected of you. Will you come up to standard? You look forward confidently or fearfully, hope for (or despair of) a good result. How you handle it is personal to you, and the more you're aware of it the better.

Expectation involves the future. Freud wrote that it was a kind of rehearsing – 'our fantasy is turned toward the future, because we rehearse for the future'. At the same time it's based on the past – what we know or think we know. The present, the act of making art right now, is poised between knowledge and expectation, and can be affected by both. Everybody experiences being right here differently; what you wrote, or thought, or said aloud, was the kind of 'talking to yourself' you usually do, and this chatter or running commentary is different for everybody. But it has some common characteristics.

What about your expectations? What can you say about them?

Up to standard

What about coming 'up to standard'? Whose standard? Expectations are not just wishes; they are also judgements. 'Once you judge,' said gestalt psychologist Fritz Perls, 'you can't experience any more, because you are now much too busy finding reasons, explanations, defence, all that crap.'

We are constantly judging ourselves, and we need to be aware of how we do so, and why.

The ball park – chatter in the head

The chatter going on in the head while you are making art is like courtroom drama, or noise from the soccer field. It can range from the one end to the other. At one end of the field is the defence, made up of people who can always find an excuse for anything that doesn't meet their personal expectations. Their chatter is full of excuses and explanations: 'Of course, this is just warming-up, I am a real beginner. I'm bad at this kind of thing. I usually use watercolours,' and so on.

The prosecution or attack, on the other hand, will be agonizing over the work, picking out all its presumed faults: 'This is not a good example of my work. Why can't I concentrate? I'll never learn. This is terrible, I have to start again. I have no idea how to draw a hand – how can people just start drawing? Why am I so stupid?' and so on. Some people play all over the field, and everybody recognizes the game.

This image of defence and attack is a good one. There's no right or wrong to it – between Matisse's armchair (he said famously that art should be as enjoyable as a good armchair) and Cézanne's black dog, every artist is somewhere on the field, and you'll know your general position very well.

Baggage

Another way of looking at the experience is in terms of baggage. We could say that we come to our art loaded down, carrying the weight of all our knowledge and expectations. Can you see yourself as more or less burdened and struggling with a heavy load? Some people are literally loaded down – they like complicated easels and all the expensive gear that is available, and that the manufacturers have convinced them is a necessary accoutrement to the successful artist.

But what is meant here by baggage is your mind's suitcases and carry-alls, that are full of all the art you have made in the past, and all the pictures you have seen and would like to emulate – your career as an artist up to now – all here, disposed around you and ready to encourage, discourage and generally interfere with your present efforts.

If you can't dispense with it, you should at least acknowledge that it's there. If only you could leave it outside, with your coat and hat. This image of the baggage is tangible and funny, one you can 'see'. In art classes you've probably met a certain student with so much stuff – some of it real enough in the form of complicated equipment, the rest mental but easy to conjure into surreal presence – that it's impossible to see past or around it; someone who sits crouched in the centre of a little fortress of cartons, knapsacks, folders and files (including perhaps even a 'presentation folio'), working away in a closed little world.

No Man's Land

Here is another working image, a really useful one. Fritz Perls used it as a metaphor for life, and it works for art just as well.

Take some paper and draw a circle in the middle. Label it SELF. Outside it, make another circle, and within it write DMZ. This stands for demilitarized zone, or NO MAN'S LAND – you can write that in there too. Outside the circles, write OTHER.

SELF stands for the me-ness, the experience of being who you are. NO MAN'S LAND or DMZ is a kind of middle zone – it is not self, yet it is not the OTHER – the outside world.

We know that region called DMZ (an older term was *complex*) very well. 'In this zone there is a fantasy life of the conscious, called 'mind', which is full of catastrophic expectations, full of fantasies,' says Perls. In it are all the experiences that seem to stand somewhere between self and the outside world, that alter your perception of it – for example, the experience of falling in love. Or, think how you feel when you walk outside after a particularly good film or concert, or wake up from a vivid dream. It's difficult, sometimes impossible, to come 'down to earth', to relate in a realistic way to the world around you. This is also the area of *prejudice* – pre-judgement: we decide to look at things in a certain way which may or may not have anything to do with what is really out there. If you have prejudice, then your relation to the world is very much disturbed and destroyed. The effect, according to Jung, 'is to isolate the subject from his environment, since instead of a real relationship to it there is now an illusory one'. Jung calls this an 'autistic condition in which one dreams a world whose reality remains forever unattainable'.

Perls speaks of 'the *trance* we live in'. Everybody can understand this model or metaphor of our existence. It is more or less, most of the time, the way we all experience the world.

You can see how it applies to art. If the senses (in this case, the sense of sight) are clouded by pre-judgement, you have difficulty in seeing what is there. Prejudices are standards, intentions and expectations, gathered over a lifetime of living in a certain culture, seeing certain pictures and being taught certain doctrines and methods and a certain aesthetic.

As you have learned already, visual perception is a complex function. You don't 'just see'. Perception has been described as being continuously in a state of active struggle between the sensory input, and the fantasizing brain which is trying to wrest control away from the senses, however much we would like to anchor our perceptions in reality. What this means and how it works is something we will be exploring later. For the present it is enough to be aware of it – and how it relates to the very real difficulty, perhaps impossibility, of seeing clearly.

In terms of the image, how can one reach through the DMZ, from SELF to OTHER? Is it possible to stand in a direct relation to the outside world, eliminate the NO MAN'S LAND between, or at least diminish it, defuse it in some way so that what is out there can be apprehended?

Why should this effort be the goal of the artist, who after all is committed to a personal, imaginative view of things? Is not the DMZ the source of creativity? These are questions which need serious consideration.

The veil

When he was a student, Giacometti had enormous difficulties in working from the model, and finally gave it up. This is his description: 'The more I studied the model, the thicker the veil between her reality and me became. At first one sees the person, but little by little all the sculptures one can imagine interpose themselves… there were too many sculptures between my model and me.' Later, he was to say to a model, 'I don't see directly any more, I see you through my knowledge.' He saw, he said, 'through the filter of the intellect'. And he drew 'precisely to reduce the thickness of that filter, and each time to come closer… to a reality which in reality does not always coincide with its appearance'.

Summing up

Just now you've been trying to pin down what it's like, as experience, to enter the creative process.

The images (ball park and baggage, DMZ and veil) describe the difficulty – how expectation and past experience seem to hinder you in getting started. And about the chatter in the mind – defence or attack. You imagined yourself starting as usual, or you actually made a drawing, and at the same time wrote a kind of running commentary on what was going on.

It might have been something like this: When I begin to make art (for example, to draw) I have expectations of myself, based on all the art I have made and all the art I have seen. I have my routines which I seem to need in order to begin, whether it is fussing about the materials and surroundings or putting on the coffee or (in class) making a series of warming-up drawings. Physically, I'm quite tense, my breathing is shallow, and I tend to complain to myself about the surroundings – the light or the paper and chalk or (if I'm a painter) the state of my brushes. I also complain in various ways about my initial progress, setting it against what I have done before, and against the beautiful art I've seen and want to emulate. Yes, I want to be better – a better artist. I reassure myself (I have routines for this too) that I'm just warming up or I'm just a beginner and doing quite well considering – and here I can bring in the external complaints if I need to, about surroundings, about materials, about time. It's all someone or something else's fault. Or I'm in dry period. All artists go through dry periods.

What hinders me?

These are images for the *experience* of beginning to make art, pictures of what it is like to embark on an act of creation. They also describe our relationship with the outside world – it is tenuous, and our ability to perceive it directly through our senses is frustrated by what we can picture, variously, as *the football field* of self-criticism, with its defence and attack, the *baggage* of standards and expectations, the *no man's land* of prejudices, pre-decisions and projections, or the veil of knowledge and memory.

Whatever the real world is, it does not necessarily correspond to our prejudices – it might not be what we would have expected. To accept this is both scary and exhilarating. Giacometti said, 'I do not work for the purpose of creating lovely pictures. Art is nothing but a means of seeing. And one continues, knowing very well that the nearer one gets to the thing, the further it moves away... It is an endless quest.'

Think about the quotation on freedom from fantasy at the beginning of this chapter (p. 71). It is actually a philosopher's statement about moral good, using art as an analogy. Applied directly to art it is even more controversial and provocative. Keep it before your mind, and consider carefully what it might mean.

It is not our eyesight, which functions well and sufficiently, or our dexterity, which is fine-tuned by years of writing and other tool-holding tasks. Whether and how we are hindered or assisted by the very nature of our perceptive faculties is the fascinating question. Can our knowledge hinder us? Can even our emotions, that may have brought us to the act of creating, get in the way?

Cupboards in the Brain

*'We do not copy that which
is before our eyes, we copy
that which by means of sight has
remained conscious in
our minds.'*

Giacometti

So far we have been exploring the artist's vision, the act of seeing, as the primary source of creativity. *Vision* means the active visual system in *its entirety*. This is the given – what we have and what we must work with. It is our access to the world and our interpretation of it. We are seeking to understand how we, as sighted human beings, choose, store and recognize what we see. And what the brain, this huge, complex, accumulated knowledge-base, gives us in return.

A strong current

Jeff Hawkins, in his book *On Intelligence*, emphasizes the fact that information in the visual cortex 'always flows in the opposite direction as well... The higher regions of your cortex send more signals "down" to your primary visual cortex than your eyes receive'.

The act of seeing reflects this conflict. What we 'know',

what Giacometti called 'this false knowledge', is a powerful current, and we are swimming against it when we strive to see more clearly, to receive more, and more accurate, information about the world.

Much of the brain's work is to store information, and make it available. For obvious reasons, that information must be sorted and categorized; we have to be able to get at it. It has been discovered recently that we recognize the category of what we see even before we identify it. Categorization isn't just instantaneous, it actually comes first. Do we decide about what we are going to see? The drawer opens and then – in goes the object. How much chance do we have of actually seeing anything in order to classify it?

When biologist and writer Jack Cohen lectures on how precepts are turned into concepts, he brings a teddy bear. At one point he holds it up and twists back its front leg, and everyone in the audience winces. The reason for their discomfort, he explains, is that they have categorized it wrongly – they have 'put it with pets and children' before they were conscious of what it was, an inanimate bit of cloth.

The cortex

The cortex or *neocortex* in the brain evolved quite recently – within the last two million years. Evolved is putting it mildly; exploded is a better description of the sudden increase in size, complexity and capability of this part of the brain, which rests on the older, 'primitive' part, sharing and in some cases taking over its functions. Think of a thickish patchwork quilt tucked over the brain – even V1 (the primary visual cortex) is not so much one large patch as a collection of smaller ones. About 10 million neurons are busy there in the dark. Picture the quilt's material as dense pile, made of tightly packed vertically stacked cells, with a surface lining, or gloss, of horizontal ones. These innumerable cells are meticulously organized and interconnected. The processing, storing and releasing of information is unimaginably complex.

Visual information enters the eyes as ever-changing patterns, and the optic nerve, a bundle of about a million fibres or axons, carries this information to the brain. As you know, cells are specific to (or fussy about) different bits of information. It is their excitement or indifference which forms and reforms the patterns. Until recently, scientists have concentrated on learning about input of sensory information – which cell receives and sends on what? And where does which kind of information go? Yet the direction of traffic back towards the senses is apparently just as heavy or heavier, and the importance of this operation (called *top-down* as opposed to *bottom-up*) is only now starting to sink in: the optic nerve is a two-way street.

Weather reports

Weather reports are biased. TV meteorologists smile when reporting a sunny day, turn their mouths down apologetically when they have to predict rain. Neurologists are also biased in favour of stored information – whatever makes sense of the chaos coming in is good; whatever interrupts the brain's work of sorting and storing information is therefore, if not bad, at least in need of organization and control, of bringing into line.

Look at the term *makes sense*. Is the brain in some way making the senses? What is this dance between what we receive and what we make of it? There are meteorologists who secretly love storms. Sometimes they appear on the media and can't hide their excitement, though they try. As artists we can love, and learn from, the mind's quirks and storms. And we might secretly love the 'storms of generosity' awaiting us out in the world. How can we understand this contradiction and use it to enhance our vision and strengthen our creativity?

How the eye moves

Let us begin again with the eyes. Our eyes do not gaze calmly at the visual field, even though this is how we experience seeing. Rather, they jerk about on short, seemingly erratic, high-velocity trajectories, or sprints. These rapid eye movements are called *saccades*.

Two to three saccades occur every second, using up about a tenth of our viewing time. During the course of a saccade there is a 'blurring' (something like that which occurs when you look fixedly at the road from a moving vehicle). The end of each saccade, like the end of a blink, signals the start of a new process of seeing. So natural vision is actually interruptive – seeing is not even a smooth succession of saccades, but a sequence of engaging and disengaging visual attention.

Vision is never really static. If the eye is fixed experimentally – prevented from making any movements at all – within a second or two everything goes black; you simply cease to see. We 'watch' even our mental imagery in this same rapid, jerky way – not just during the well-known REM stages of dreaming, but whenever we conjure up a visual image.

All this saccadic motor activity is involuntary and unnoticed. Yet the direction of a saccade is never random; it seems to be determined before the start. It is involuntary in the sense of being unconscious; at the same time, it is predetermined, or 'chosen' on some level of preference that does not require the 'extravagance' of conscious awareness. We have worked with attention, and know that we can control attention consciously. We cannot control our saccades.

Or can we? Later we will get back to the saccadic mechanism as it relates to the corticular processes, and explore what might be done about it.

Scan paths

The saccades' trajectory seems to zip here and there with little correspondence to the contours of form – yet whenever you look at a familiar object, such as an upright human face, your saccades will trace the same predetermined, repetitive route. What is interesting is not just that saccades have these preferred pathways (called *scan paths*), but that these pathways are forever revisited. Each time you recognize something, you'll scan it on the same well-trodden route.

Saccades are an outward, measurable sign of what is, as yet, not fully understood. We remember what we have seen, and the brain is locked into seeing it again in a particular way. How do we teach ourselves these paths? How do we learn to recognize and understand what is seen? What happens in the brain, so that the memory is ready to prompt and direct our eyes along these habitual pathways?

The invariant representation

What we perceive does not come from our senses alone. Take a familiar face. As you sit across from a friend in a café, and look at her, many patterns are being sent from your eyes to your brain. Your friend is chatting, nodding, eating, turning away to speak to someone else. Her face is definitely not staring fixedly in one direction as in a photograph. Yet whatever the angle, you continue to recognize her; you don't seem to need a single, head-on view. What is happening?

Your eyes scan her face in predetermined saccades. Information is transmitted to V1 to be sorted and relayed to higher areas. Recognition is widely distributed in the cortex, but face recognition is specific to a particular area – the *fusiform gyrus*. Here, the cells selective for this face are activated, and stay active as long as the face is in view. They exist as a template or pattern, a stable cell assembly, devoted to this face. It is called an *invariant representation*. How did it come about? What information does it contain?

Traffic on the visual highway

In looking at a familiar face, you perceive a kind of combination – what your senses are telling you, and what your brain is telling you based on memory. A persuasive story of how it works goes something like this.

Patterns occurring together, when you are exposed to them often enough, begin to stick together. For now, think of it as a kind of *glue*. A pattern at 'eye level' can be very simple – say your friend's right eyelid seen at a certain angle. Specific cells in your retina respond to this spatially specific boundary and pass it on as a sequence, repetitively, as often as it is seen. Cells in V1 devoted to this orientation receive it, surrounding cells are activated, and the information moves as a sequence on up the cognitive highway.

You know your friend's face. As information is passed on, these detailed, fast-changing sequences so often received can be collapsed into more simple, slow-changing ones. *Inhibitory* cells decide you 'know all that already', and prevent the clutter of unnecessary patterning (you don't need to register her eyelid to know who she is). What is left moves on towards the top of the hierarchy. (Remember, we are pre-wired to embrace this configuration as a *face* anyway.) Along the way, missing information is filled in and ambiguities suppressed – only one alternative gets through. Meanwhile, the stable sequences are taking over further and further down the hierarchy, the more often the cells are exposed. To give another example: when you were learning to read, your sequences laboured far up the highway as individual letters. Later this amount of detail was unnecessary and words, even phrases, looped ever lower as stable assemblies.

There can be U-turns in traffic if something untoward or unexpected is reported, and more information needs to be picked up from further back (thrown into the back seat) before driving on. And with the invariant in place, *top-down* traffic streams down towards your eyes. You recoup towards the retina and end in the saccade, the jerky movement right on target at your friend's eyelid.

The brain must compromise, and downplays or ignores what does not fit its expectations. It interrupts, rejects, weighs what's probable. Small changes that occur during the saccades are ignored in favour of what is already known. It's almost as if a picture of your friend, supplied by you, is slapped over what you are looking at and everything is made to fit. This description of the highway is a persuasive story which may well turn out to be true.

Anticipation

fMRIs show that sight is anticipated, with the cells of the template or invariant representation firing up in readiness for what we expect to see. This was happening as you waited for your friend to arrive. You recognize her because of a representation, a sequence of patterns that corresponds to her face, and in a very real way anticipates what you see.

This works for us because stored memory about the world corresponds quite well to the way the world behaves. From past experience the brain can predict fairly accurately (and usually unthinkingly) what will happen next (at least, what will happen in the brain).

Imagine getting up and going outside. Imagine your movements in rising from the chair and how your feet will step across the floor, and imagine the detailed appearance of the street, its 'fit' into the neighbourhood.

Whether you actually move or not, everything you imagined (everything you anticipated) has readied you, and if you could look inside your brain you'd have seen the involved cell systems and sequences firing off in preparation. Things usually go right, and we expect them to. Maybe it is only when things go wrong that we notice how dependent we are on this smooth, temporal progression of senses, motor skills and orientation. The rake across the path or the third step that wasn't there are extraordinary. They remind us that in the overwhelming majority of instances, we do 'know' what is going to happen. There is a kind of workable complacency in our lives from day to day. To go back to an earlier image, we're still on the roof, but we aren't that aware of being at the edge of it.

Ideal Form

Invariant representation is a modern term and means something close to Plato's *Ideal Form*. Plato was interested in how we can possibly identify the common, characteristic elements of an object when all we experience are incomplete, varying aspects of it. He concluded that Forms pre-existed, and that as eternal souls we knew them in their timeless perfection. Here, in the darkness of our earthly life, we see no more than imperfect and flickering reflections cast against the wall of the cave. But we recognize them because of the Forms we remember from another plane. That they exist is now pretty much indisputable, though their origin is here in the brain, in the way it is structured.

At the beginning of this book I said that sight pre-exists within us, because the visual system is structured to start to see. We are born fully formed and not yet downloaded, organizationally predisposed to the most likely outcome. In this sense you could say we come to our lives with a built-in 'collective unconscious', an archetypal mechanism with a long past and a bias towards what is probably going to happen to us. Then we start to build up our categories (like the wrong one for Jack Cohen's teddy bear). Just like the baby gnu who can distinguish his mother from a hyena within ten minutes of birth, *but only if he has seen both*, we need the world's information even though we already 'know' what to do with it.

Generals and particulars

What about art? Is this Ideal Form, this distillation of imperfections and change into permanent clarity, the property of art? If it is, then to make art is to represent or embody Ideal

Forms, and thus reimpose permanence and perfection on the world. Art becomes the visible expression of invariance and constancy. Something resonates here – everyone has had the experience of coming out of a solo exhibition and seeing the world as the artist saw it. Artists 'teach us to see' in a very persuasive way.

The brain, as we have learned, chooses to keep in its store of memory everything it deems necessary and to discard whatever is deemed superfluous, fleeting and incomplete. The invariant representation is indeed *are-presentation*. It is dependable and allows us to anticipate and get on with our lives. It has to be general rather than particular.

All sorts of questions come up. What are the sources of art and creativity? The world of the creative imagination is surely within, and accessible to us, in the storehouse of invariant representations. Are we bound to the structure of these invariants, and is it our purpose as artists to re-create them?

Mysteries within and without

Might it not be naïve to settle for this, let alone strive for it? The problem here is getting at the truth, and the truth is many-faceted. The truth of the invariant is necessarily impoverished, and the truth of the world is thankfully predictable. What now? I'd opt for the world, or at least keep an open mind. For all its tendency to be predictable, it might have some surprises, and the edge of the roof might be closer than we think.

As an artist, your task is to choose and be attentive to whatever truth you can get at. In a very real sense you are your memory. But your creative nourishment comes from the edge, and out there is the real, with its mysteries.

Poet-artist-mystic William Blake called them *minute particulars*. As for invariants (he called them *General Forms*), he renounced them indignantly, calling them 'Swell'd & bloated General Forms repugnant to the Divine'. The goal of the artist according to Blake was to 'protect minute particulars, every one in their own identity'.

What does it mean to protect the particulars? And what is identity?

The entrapment of creativity

We have been looking at the predetermination – it could even be called the *entrapment* – of vision. Take a minute or so to consider how this applies to your art, your creativity. Though the source and nourishment of vision must be the seen world, the very process of learning to see involves structuring that world and responding to it in a certain way. The way we see is common to the species; we can communicate, and therefore must assume that we share a close, workable idea of the world. And we're locked into it. We learned sight so early on that any idea of unlearning, of returning to a different or somehow clearer way of seeing the world, is surely naïve and self-defeating.

Yet for you, in practice (this is happening and you know about it) there's this continuous struggle to see better and understand more – and this hindrance, this work, this sense of being blocked or entrapped, is part of the artist's life. This quest, this despair, this never being quite satisfied.

Take a mirror and make a drawing of part of your face. Choose the most familiar feature – the eye. Draw one eye.

The essence of the entrapment

With your first look, you stepped into the essence of the entrapment. Of all the objects in the world, the face is the most familiar, and the eye its most familiar feature. It's inevitable that 'seeing' the eye in the face is going to involve top-down information of the most determined, no-nonsense kind. Your scan path was not conscious, but you can be sure it was well signposted and slavishly followed. The invariant came cascading forward to meet you with its stored information about this face and this eye, so that what you were 'seeing' was in a true sense already seen.

What were your conscious reactions in making this drawing?

There is a funny kind of complacency in looking at the well known – and a kind of relief as well. You'd probably have noticed this as you settled in: 'All right, here's something I know all about.' You may have learned about 'how to draw the eye', so you have some handy techniques and could apply them. Little things like where the pupil is placed – as an artist, your idea of the eye probably includes the knowledge that the pupil is usually partly hidden by the upper lid. If however you hadn't yet learned this, your eye-invariant probably top-downed a pupil smack in the centre – which is the way you drew it. The representation was more pushy than what you actually saw.

Set up the following experiment. Use two mirrors or a friend. Draw the eye from the side. Check your reactions as you draw.

This exercise should evoke more interest, and chances are you felt somewhat excited, as the new view engaged your attention. Familiar, and at the same time less familiar as an object to draw. Where did you place the pupil this time? Look again.

Now we could ask ourselves what is it about the pupil that makes it hard to place, and why should the eye-invariant have the pupil misplaced to start with? What is it about the pupil, and what does the pupil share with other objects (what would they be?) in wanting to be drawn wrong? These are fascinating questions.

In drawing the model, as in drawing any familiar object, the invariant takes over, or tries to, all the time. When it comes to the human body, any idea that the inner representation is some kind of quintessential 'ideal' just can't be right. It isn't that one wants, consciously, to smooth out, generalize and prettify. More is involved.

You can probably think of examples. The standing pose, or the reclining pose seen side-on, are drawn longer, thinner, more flattened, because this powerful inner representation overrides what is seen. The head in practically any pose is drawn more erect – we 'know' the head is supposed to be on top of the body, and we know this with a vengeance.

Easy and difficult

If you've drawn from the model you can remember your reaction to different poses. A pose is 'easy' or 'difficult' (and if it is very difficult you might even decide to move). *Difficult* means unfamiliar – 'I have to look' – and *easy* means familiar – 'I can use my knowledge'. You prefer one or the other, depending on your temperament. One model I encountered called himself an 'extreme model' and wanted to get into all sorts of contortions with ropes and poles. The idea was to make things as difficult as possible. On the other hand, a certain pose (known disparagingly as 'the little mermaid') keeps recurring among inexperienced models in Denmark – the model sitting demurely with legs tucked up under her. Which would you prefer to draw?

With an 'easy' pose, there is that sense of relief – that you know all about it – coupled with a conscious or unconscious slackening of focus. To bring such a pose to the attention requires a real effort and is often doomed to failure. It is as though the brain is bent on sabotage – as Giacometti said, 'I can't see you any more. I see you through my knowledge.'

Objects are obvious

The world has its structure, and how we perceive the world has its structure, and they do not always coincide. We apply the brain's structure to the world. It is time to look at how we do this, and what it means to us as artists.

Look at the visual field as if you were a mover and were going to make an inventory: check out the furniture. Then choose one piece. Keep it in mind as you continue to read.

Our perception separates the visual world into *categories*, and within these categories into *objects*.

Furniture is a category; the chair, or whatever you chose, is an object. This is obvious, but look at what is being done. We organize the world into fixed lumps of stuff, big lumps which we then further organize into smaller ones. What constitutes a lump? How does a lump stay together? How does it all work?

Lumps of stuff

The German term for this is *Prägnatz*, which means 'goodness of form'. What form do we perceive as *good*?

A *good* lump of stuff has visual attributes which our brain has decided should be respected, boundaries which separate it from its background and from other lumps. See whether the chair (or other object you chose) checks with these attributes:

- Closure – the object ends off in some visual way
- Connectedness – it seems to hold together
- Convexity – it bulges or extends towards me
- Contour – its boundaries or edges continue all the way round. In other words, it's spatially and visually a whole.

Though you can agree that, yes, these attributes refer to the chair, think how much they are dependent on you as the perceiver, on your decision that the chair has an independent existence, and a fixed, continuing existence in this ever-changing world. Coherence means glue – the glue of your idea of it as one object.

Cross two pencils, or a pen and a pencil, on the table.

What have you got? A visual boundary and a connectedness, and a bulge towards you, and edges that are, at least visually, continuous from where you sit. But without that glue, that idea of wholeness inside your brain, they aren't an object. You don't respect them as fixed with a fixed existence. Subjectively, they aren't a whole.

Sets and subsets

Within your world of perceived objects there are of course groupings – sets and subsets dividing off almost endlessly. Even the main categorical group (furniture) fits into higher, more global groups – like the word I used, *inventory*, under which the mover could have listed many other household items besides furniture. The subsets of furniture are chair, sofa and so forth.

Visual psychologists have termed the main grouping (furniture) the *tree* (though they are not very consistent, putting the root at the top and sometimes calling the limbs *children*), and the places where its subsets branch off they call *joints* or *nodes*. Under the *tree* heading (*furniture*) the nodes could be specific and connect only to it, not to each other, so if one of them (*chair*) was broken off perceptually – a disjoint – it would have enough coherence to be seen as an object in itself. *Chair* has nodes with subsets like seat, back, legs, cushion. The *cushion's* subsets include its cover; the *cover's* subsets, its textured or patterned surface; and the *surface's* subsets are its visibly discrete markings, for example dots or stripes.

The given

This is all obvious but, as we will see, of extreme importance to us as artists. We perceive the world in a very strict way, according to seemingly unalterable rules, and we learned to do this very early on. Actually, it's the crucial part of learning to see. Humans are insatiably curious, and as we grew up we gained expertise in categorizing and assigning objects. We learned out of necessity and also through devotion – everybody knows how many subsets of subsets can be mastered by a really devoted expert, be it in computers, cookery, football or keeping bees.

As artists, we have to go with the given, like everyone else. We can't turn back the clock to a time in infancy before we did this to ourselves, and we can't change the basic rules. Or can we?

The mind's eye

Before we attempt to answer this, let's return to the *invariant representation*, the concept or ideal form inside the brain. Plato's example of an ideal form was a couch – the ideal couch which incorporated all couchness.

Choose an object as invariant. Name and imagine it.

There is a jar on the table in front of me so I'll choose *jar*. Through repeated exposure to jars, my brain has stored an encoded pattern of this object. I hardly glance at the one on the table, because my memory knows all about jar and can recall a visual image of it any time I want. Even now, as I sit here, I'm associating, picturing how poor little Piglet tried to tell Christopher Robin about the Heffalump – that it was 'like an enormous big nothing – like a jar'. Which in a funny way sums up the essence of the invariant.

This invariant is in its place, readily available, an object with a name. It is also, somehow, seen – it is an image in the mind's eye. But what is the mind's eye?

Pictures or propositions?

Seeing pictures in your mind is called a *quasi-perceptual experience*, and strangely enough there is still argument as to whether there are actual pictures in there, laid down in the cells. Could an object you are looking at be identified by the pattern of brain activity? On a small scale, the activation of columns of orientation cells has been shown to replicate the edges of objects seen – and visual recall of an object (seeing it in the mind's eye) activates the same cortical area as does seeing it. *Pictorialists*, adherents of the idea of 'real' pictures, point out that these images have a *spatial property*, that if we imagine moving across a pictured location, there is a measurable time-lapse equal to the imagined distance. They argue that this proves the physical existence of a map of some sort.

Propositionalists dispute this – according to them, the imagination is quite capable of asking 'What would it be like if?' and supplying temporal-spatial answers. Retinal 'maps' (the field as received by photocells at the back of the eye) are two-dimensional, flat, while imagined images are experienced in depth, and this argues for a fundamental difference between them. It's like the difference between *phosphenes*, or *afterimages*, and mental imagery. Phosphenes are the lights you see when you push at your closed eyelids; and *afterimages* are negative images which persist when you have gazed at, for example, a black patch, car lights or a sunset. They are involuntary while mental images are intentional. And if we project an afterimage onto a surface, it stays the same size wherever the surface is located, whereas a mental image would accommodate itself.

⌒∽⊕ *To test this (it's called Emmet's law), try staring at a black shape on a white ground for at least 30 seconds. Then look at white paper close by, and then at a (white) wall further off.*

Reaching for and rotating a real object, and imagining the same actions with an imagined one, are also quite different experiences: in the latter case rather jerky, like a movie made up of too few stills.

We do not normally confuse the imagined and the visually seen, though there are borderlines, waking dreams and hallucinations, spooky thresholds where they seem to overlap. *Eidetic* images (extremely 'real' mental images that can be intentional) can be experienced as 'out there', and are extraordinarily vivid. Most children have them and in some adults the ability persists. On another scale but no less 'visual' than dreams or day-dreams or pictured images, are verbal or 'literary images', which neurologists do not classify as sensory images at all, because they are conjured up by words alone, and therefore should be called something else.

⌒∽⊕ *Think of a phrase of a poem – something you have by heart, be it Byron or Dylan or a nursery rhyme.*

A literary image can be extremely (and visually) evocative; at the same time it is inextricably glued to language – to the exact words it is expressed in, the non-appreciation of which accounts for the general failure of trying to teach, explain or 'appreciate' poetry at school. Consider Lowell's lines about a painting, with the sun's illumination *stealing like the tide across a map/ to his girl solid with yearning.*

The Ripeness of Sight

What we worship in the human body is more than its beautiful shape; it is the inward flame that seems to illuminate it, to shine through it.

Rodin

Rodin entered a kind of stillness just before he began to draw. He would wait for a moment, what he called the *moment de pause*, until his sight *matured*. Only then did hebegin. What did he mean by this ripening of sight?

You can use a large mirror and sit or stand so you can see your whole body. Or look at someone else – here, or later in a drawing class with a model. It doesn't matter what the pose is (yours or a friend's or the model's) so long as you have a human object to look at and, later, to draw from.

Object-making

As you look, your perception is already at work, categorizing and object-making.

This time, acknowledge what you are doing consciously. Be aware of how you are dividing and subdividing – think of the body as a tree with subsets branching off from nodes, and of other subsets from further nodes. Think of each part as an object.

Where do you place the nodes? What objects do you see?

The body is a great example of how we perceive objects, sets and subsets. And how we perceive where they leave off – their boundaries. Another term for node is *joint*, and for a reason. Here at a joint, just as in a tree, another part connects. It is natural that your idea of the body creates objects out of the parts attached by joints. How often in looking at a complex pose (the 'difficult' pose mentioned earlier) do you think, 'how in the world do all these parts connect'? It's normal to want to start by comparing and sorting out and piecing together as well as you can. There is a good chance you have learned the rules of proportion and have been encouraged to think and work this way.

Rodin's insight tells us there is another way – a way of perceiving the body as a unity.

The body as object

Earlier, you made some drawings without using line, to see whether you could come a little closer to what is really out there without abstracting. Now you are going to try something else: whether it's possible to draw without further object-making – without identifying nodes, branches and subsets. You may be even less sure about this one. But the idea is interesting to play with and the results can be surprising indeed.

You can't get away from the body as object – this is, after all, what you are staring at. The body as a whole fulfils the requirements of objecthood by being a lump of stuff separated from its background, with fairly regular edges. It has convexity (sits in space) and you expect it to stay there and be itself for some time. Could this object be perceived as an object without subsets, indivisible? This is what Rodin meant. But how can it be done? Think for a moment about what truths you could record about it, while still keeping its unity.

The truth of size

First of all, and maybe so obvious you wouldn't bother to list it, is its size. This is an attribute you could record, if you had paper big enough. Mostly, artists don't worry about size. Sculptors doing busts and figures might respect it – working in three dimensions they are nearer to straight representation, and this includes the possibility of making things 'life-sized'. But in making pictures it doesn't seem to matter. You can't paint a mountain or a building that big anyway. It has to do with practicalities. The portrait, like the bust, is a special instance.

In my work I draw a lot of babies, and here size has its place. Premature babies, in particular, are measured – their exact length (which can be down to 18cm/7in) is important, sometimes vital, to get right. We hold babies, and too small or too large on the page is harder to accept. As for a portrait, an observer would stand about the same distance away as from a person – a culturally determined, domestic distance acknowledging presence. So the artist usually chooses to paint the head to cover the same amount of the field you'd experience looking at someone 'face to face'. It is a choice, and artists can choose otherwise – the oversized portrait is now common.

Even given big pieces of paper, drawing up to actual size can be hard. Again for practical reasons, most of the surfaces we've used to write or draw on are small. It's about habit and dexterity; we can make closely gathered, exact marks and keep things under control, and draw as if we were writing a list or a letter. Much of the talk about 'freedom' in drawing and painting is often just talk about size – about the physical act of swinging your arm widely, losing the restraint that is necessary when working on a small scale.

But in general we are perfectly satisfied with small, sometimes very small, representations of people and other objects – we're accustomed to a field of vision in which space is already miniaturized no matter how close something is to your face. In drawing and painting, the concern is the relationships within the image itself.

So you probably won't draw this body to size. But size is an attribute, a 'truth' you could keep in mind, and be aware of when it's your choice not to go there.

The truth of density

Another less obvious truth is density. The body you are looking at is solid; information about it stops at the surface and, except for a little way into the eyes, and an even shallower transparency of the skin, you can't see past the surface.

Think for a moment about the difference between *container* and *content*.

Make a little doodle line drawing, the outline of a ball or a box, and then beside it make a dark mass the same shape.

The first drawing represents the *container*, the second, the *content*. Usually, people draw containers using line. Here, we want to pay attention to the weight and solidity of what's inside.

As we now know, the brain loves line, and line is perfectly capable of describing content, if that content has been seen and understood. Our visual system works this way and perceives, as we have seen, linear closures or boundaries descriptive of objects we recognize. But it might be very useful to pay attention to content on its own, and to say something direct about it.

Say it out loud

Drawing the content, rather than outlining it, is a bit like the difference between thinking something and speaking it out loud. You may go around thinking something vaguely and repetitively for years; only by saying it out loud do you realize what you've been doing. Speech, like art, is a means of external storage and contemplation, and speaking out loud is a way to test and clarify thought, to take responsibility for it. Speaking out loud means being committed to what you say – physically, with your muscle and breath. You are externalizing, and having an objective look at, what you think. Rodin said, 'My drawings are only a way of testing myself.' When you draw the content, it's your way of speaking aloud, of 'saying it'.

Drawing content is also a very good way of getting things true the first time, whereas line can be guesswork and will probably need correcting. If you start somewhere inside the object, be it a box, tin can, apple or model, you can begin with the truth and not have to rely on guesswork at all.

*Look toward the object (the body) and make
a drawing, without using line, of its content. Use
pressed charcoal or conté or a brush and wash. Record
its density.*

It is difficult to draw this way. You might even, before you
could stop yourself, have sketched in some tentative outlines
to guide you, which you could then 'fill in'. Or imagined them
– you know that the brain was telling you to see them.

Mass

By beginning inside, you were in a sense accumulating
mass, at least the idea of mass. This object is a mass, and you
can think of amassing its representation on your page. Think
of heaping up rather than of drawing. In The Natural Way to
Draw, Nicolaides wrote, 'Work, as nearly as possible, like a
sculptor modelling in clay.' His exercises on beginning at the
core of the form are an excellent way of training your eye to
see as Rodin saw, to ripen your sight and comprehend the
whole. I have taught them for many years and almost
forgotten where they came from. Now I suddenly understand
their underlying meaning in connection to the brain's
tenacious object-making.

If you were a sculptor representing this body out of clay,
you would have to begin somewhere inside, and to begin
somewhere inside you must learn to ripen your sight.

*Look toward the figure, using the sculptor's
kind of attention, and intuitively search out a place
to begin: here is where the sculptor would have to
start heaping up the clay. Then draw by adding to this*

*first mark, piling on marks extending outward in
all directions. Draw keeping the sculptor's attention
in mind.*

Of course the surface of the paper is flat: we can't kid
ourselves that we are making a mound; yet we are able to
work somewhere at the perceptual boundary between depth
and the illusion of depth, and to experience the tiny amount
of depth as real – which it is, because we are literally 'piling
on' chalk or paint, and where we observe that the form is
bulkiest and densest, the chalk or paint is most thickly layered
and laid down.

This is saying truths out loud – truths about solidity,
density, weight. Each stroke you lay down speaks about how
dense this object is; each mark rests on the one before, heaped
up towards you and outwards, towards the surface and closure
of the form.

You may find this kind of drawing so strange as to be almost
impossible. How can one make soft marks somewhere in the
centre without first, at least tentatively, 'sketching' in an
outline? But out-lines or guide-lines – even tentative, sketchy
ones – mean separating, object-making. And they cannot be
trusted to be true.

It's a good idea to halt your drawings in process, early on,
and look at them. Make sure they began inside the core of
density. If you are still making furtive outlines, it is somewhat
senseless to proceed.

*Begin a few drawings, just the beginnings. Try
writing NO LINES on the page, and add the words
CORE/DENSITY – a signpost to keep you on track.*

In drawing this way you can actually experience, through your own hand and arm, the depth of what you are drawing, as you force form away from you by sheer muscular pressure.

A good, solid black

Rodin said, 'I try to see the figure as mass, as volume.' These drawings should be visible mass – a good, solid black, and blackest in the part you perceived as the most dense – the part where the sculptor would have started massing the clay. If your drawings appear billowy or partly transparent, with 'air holes' here and there, you need to return to the beginning and work more solidly (really solidly) outward. Remember Giacometti: 'The mass has an energy that is turned in upon itself, violently compressed around a central core.'

If you have never drawn this way before, it might be hard to decide where to begin. Something called 'the core of density' is fantasy, isn't it? It's not visible, not on the surface. Yet this is the closest possible image for what you are trying to do – to perceive something as a single object and draw it that way. An apple has a core or centre. So does anything else perceived as an object, however complicated. Certainly a human figure, even an elongated one. The sculptor, working on a long complex figure, might have to build some sort of armature first so it doesn't fall apart.

Where would the core be in the pose you are looking at? It need not be the feet even in a standing pose – Inuit soapstone sculpture, for example (the original, not the later ones intended for sale) was made to be held, and passed from hand to hand. In most poses the core, the centre of density, will be somewhere low in the torso.

⟋⟍◯ *Make another drawing, beginning inside, and*
building it up, solidly, from a core of density. Then put it
on the wall.

From a distance your drawing should look solid, with
(naturally, as it is solid black) no surface features or details.

One, or many?

The idea is to see whether you can perceive the body as one
object rather than a connected series of anatomical bits. The
body is indeed complex, and the usual way of working with
complexity is by subdividing it into nodes and subsets, by
object-making. The body is made up of lots of parts connected
in particular ways, and surely the more anatomy you know the
better you can tackle them and get them all right. This isn't
even an argument in most drawing instruction – it's a given.
You can use your own body to test this.

⟋⟍◯ *As you sit there in your body, try a few different*
perceptions of it. Think of yourself as 'you'. Where is
your core of density? Think of background or not-you
all around about. Think of you as different from
background – compressed, consolidated, warmer and
somehow more vital. Think of your total weight, of
being held solidly inside your skin. Now think of just
one part of your body – maybe your head, looking
down at the rest. Where is the node between head and
everything else?

Think of some other part, for example, your thumb and
how it connects to your hand. Where's the node?

Maybe you can think of some part of yourself you don't like or which hurts, or hurt once in the past. Is there an imaginary node between it and the rest?

Don't think of an elephant

There might well be a node there, and it might be more than imaginary. Pain can cause disassociation (you don't want to go there) and disassociation can literally cut off circulation and prevent healing. It's like the elephant the Chinese healer told the patient not to think about when taking the medicine. A kind of rigid, negative attention.

If this makes any sense in your experience, try thinking of the node as a tight piece of string, and see whether in imagination you can loosen or untie it.

Now return to yourself as a unity, an inseparable you.

Extending

The dense, black drawings are speaking about the body as one object, not many objects. When you record (say aloud) the truth of density, beginning right in the centre, you can't make different objects out of the one – you have to perceive it as a unity. Your drawings are the witness to how you have seen.

But what about details? This approach is all very well for a big, black figure, but how do you continue? The way is to extend, gradually.

You have already done this, maybe right to the surface. The way forward (and outward) to the boundaries of the figure should be continuous: you extend the marks until you get there, and then stop. The trick for not getting involved in subsets of objects is to go back to the core of density *every single time*. There is no easy way past the perceptual nodes unless you gear up from the start and charge through at one go. Remember that nodes (joints) and objects (head, arm, hand and so on) are subjective signposts your brain imposes, a way – one way – to organize reality.

Practically, you have to return to the core after every stroke. From there extend outward in one stroke, not lifting your chalk or brush. You can also use your hands – it's a great way of being in touch with what you are seeing.

No matter how complex, the body is a unity. From where you are looking, the arms may be in front of the torso. In the completed drawing they'll comprise more chalk or paint overlaid on the torso and won't even be discernible. But what you can't see is still there. And your work of gradually extending that arm through from the core of density right to the fingertips is not lost visibly, either – the direction, the texture of your stroke still lends its interpretation to the surface. A drawing in which you just flatly filled in the area displaced by the body, as if you were copying a shadow, would look flat. In your drawing, inside those intense, woolly, overworked blacks, can be found depth, weight and direction.

What about extending where you can't see it? Say into the leg partly hidden behind the other? If you are working like a sculptor, you will extend according to the information you have. When you look at a leg crossed by an arm, you don't decide there must be two separate bits of leg – you know it's whole. The brain does the filling-in based on visual cues and experience. Your visual cues tell you about the continuous flow of the form, and that flow is like a river – sometimes hidden by trees or an outcropping, but ever there, ever flowing.

Filling-in

Here your brain is definitely on your side. It hates ambiguity. Using the 'noise' of the background, even if the information is broken and incomplete, the brain is able to supply what is missing to make a coherent, understandable contour, and is doing this constantly. No one is quite sure how this mechanism (called *filling-in*) works, or where it takes place, but it is part of the top-down traffic in the cortex, meeting and making sense of what is coming in from the retina.

Staying on the paper

Lifting the chalk or brush (or your hand) from the paper breaks the perceptual flow. We'll be looking later on at where, how and why you might decide to break off. Right now, make a rule – keep your marks steadily on the paper. Lift only when you return to the core of density to extend once more.

When you have extended in all directions, right out to where the object ends, you'll have a black, dense drawing. No on-surface details will show through. But you'll have drawn to the surface – your chalk or brush or even better, your hands, will have touched it, there where your long and longer strokes ended, where the form ended.

Make one or two extended drawings. Begin every stroke in the core of density. Use your hands, at least towards the completion of the drawing, when you have lots of chalk on the page and your hands are black anyway. If you are using wash, a wet cloth held in the hand will bring you more closely in touch with the surface.

Accurate closures

You may be dissatisfied with the boundaries. Yet you can be as accurate as you like. What you began with, there inside, has its truth, and there's no reason why this truth-making can't continue out to the edges. Drawing like this is an excellent way of avoiding all the fuss about *proportion*; your chances are good that the proportion will take care of itself. Proportion means comparison and comparison means compartmentalizing – the construction of mental compartments, which is object-making. As you complete the drawing you can attend to precise, truthful closures arrived at from the inside.

For Rodin, ripeness of sight meant seeing wholeness, perceptively taking hold of the one object in its unity with a reflexive, almost instantaneous grasp. Drawing from the core or centre trains you to begin where you can't separate the figure into different parts; extending gradually trains you to stay with this truth of unity while you complete the drawing. By making the black, massed drawings you 'put your money where your mouth is' – you say out loud that you saw that unity.

Speak in a whisper

It's all very well to represent a whole object when you use solid black, but what happens when you want to draw in detail? Details could well insist on being objects. Is it possible to keep this idea of unity? You'll find that there is a logical sequence: just as the sculptor, having constructed a dense figure, can work on its surfaces in more and more detail, you can work on the surfaces of your figure too, as soon as it is solidly there.

However, you'll need to express the whole figure more

lightly. In the image of speaking out loud, the black drawings are high-decibel growls. *Here I am, heavy and massive, compressed around my core and filling up my space with absolute authority. I am one object.* A drawing can, while speaking aloud, communicate its unity in a lower voice, even a whisper.

> *Make another drawing in the same way, still working from the central core, still without line, still extending to the boundaries. This time do it as lightly as possible.*

You may need to make several drawings, because the first one (or the first few) will get too dark. Think of the whole figure as seen through fog or smoke, so that it is almost not there at all. Use soft charcoal or a pale wash, and use your hands or a cloth just as soon as there is enough tone laid down.

Another problem is that details 'happen to' appear. As soon as the form is lighter, your brain's desire to object-make, to separate the body into parts, comes swarming in. Don't succumb; use your sculptor's attention, stubbornly building your solid form outward in light grey. Stave off surface details for later, when there is form to work on, just as the sculptor would.

> *Make another very light, smoky drawing. Just as before, work outwards from the dense core and extend to the surfaces. Make accurate closures. This time, be aware of depth, and begin to push back areas furthest away, using the pressure of your hand. As you push, you will automatically apply more tone.*

Pushing into depth

This kind of drawing could easily turn into a mechanical draw-to-formula exercise. You check out which part of the form is furthest from you ('Let's see now, the further away it is, the blacker I have to make it') and you make that area black, intermediate areas less black, and the foremost areas light. You could draw away by rule and get a rather layered, flat effect, as if the model were made up of a series of crude, stereoscopic plates.

So don't think *dark and light*, but engage your tactile sense, and think about *pushing into depth*. Darks and lights are the result, not the intent. Your intent is to model, to record depth.

Already, as you've worked with solid form, you were moving softly into a sense of three dimensions – working forward and backward as well as outward towards the sides of the form. This is not just fantasy, because you are physically involved. You can experience the muscular force, the push, in your arm and hand. As you record the form furthest from you, press deeper into the page. This pressure results in darker tone. Fortunately the eye reads darker areas on modelled form as more distant (this is called the *Appelles' principle* after the Greek who first noticed it) and your resultant drawing will have an appearance of depth.

Tactile modelling

The real reason for working through these modelled drawings is perceptual: you are learning, by drawing, how to manipulate form. And you really are building as you progress from the centre, piling on the chalk. Sometimes it will be most natural to use your hands, which are black by now anyway, to touch the chalky mass and push it around – you are physically pressing it into the page as you bear down on it with your weight, and shove the chalk against the surface. So it is not a case of thinking about making some areas blacker; to do so mechanically opens the door to object-making – divisive, sequential drawing – even though you may have started with a well-voiced, complete figure.

Think of this work as getting your hands into the drawing, as handling form. Obviously Michelangelo did not draw with light and shade in mind. His intent was to find out about form. As you draw you can ask yourself: 'Could it be possible to use this form as a basis for reconstructing the object?' Would someone, looking at it, be able to build this figure as a sculpture, in real depth?

Looking at the drawing from a distance (or squinting at it) will tell you immediately whether it works in terms of depth. A very pale area might 'jump out' at the observer. This means, in terms of form, it ought to lie deeper in space. Usually this dislocation happens with the face and, with a female model, the breasts. It's obvious these are catchy areas: they get special treatment on the page because the brain has decided they have significance – they have become objects.

You can rely on this intuitive reading of depth in terms of tone, and use it to push any jumpy areas back into line. For the sculptor, face and breasts are continuous with larger forms.

Rodin called his late drawings 'the result of his sculpture'. As an old man Henry Moore said, 'Drawing is everything. All the sculptors who have been any good are great draughtsmen. Nowadays, I do nothing but draw.'

Light and the surface

Modelled form is not dependent on light and has nothing to do with incidental cast shadows or what is called 'shading'. An overhead light makes the surface appear lighter where it falls, but may or may not describe the truth of the form. The model is the same whether the light is moved, or turned off altogether. It's as if you were analysing form not by eye but by touch, trying to discover the shape of a stone hidden in a bag of darkness.

Remember the drawings you made earlier, with the idea of delving into and under surfaces. This is the way Michelangelo drew. His forms recede into darkness, withdrawing from a diffused light which seems to have come from his own eyes. The 'light source' is the artist's own gaze, the artist's proximity.

Make another drawing. Work as before, taking time to build up a pale grey, dense form. Only then, when you are satisfied that the mass is lightly but solidly represented, begin to model, thinking of your chalk as a rough tool, used to gouge areas out, shove them back into space, press edges away where the forms round off out of sight. Be careful on the surfaces of larger forms; do not cut too deeply. Each form should lie within its space, the closest part softly held in the light of your gaze.

Then, your tool finer and sharper, make the precise incisions that give the surface its detail and accuracy. The slit where finger lies against finger, the meeting of the lips, the hair's mass carefully slid under and defined – these final particulars are like punctuation, and they'll make the drawing tick with life.

Seeing whole

It is hard to stay long enough with the build-up of form. Your purpose in actually drawing this first stage is to witness that you have seen it – seen the human form as one object. The trouble is that, given the temptation of surface trivia, nobody wants much to stay with the intent, the careful work of beginning at truth and extending the truth.

The voice of the drawing can eventually fade away to a whisper, a drift of smoke; but it is still there, saying that you have seen the whole. Rodin in his mastery saw wholeness and recorded it in his drawings, even though he did not build them up physically as you have done. He drew his 'famous contour' with swift authority *because* he had already seen.

Working with a model in this way is rewarding, because in a class you can also work up to size, with a variety of poses and at your own pace. But the human body is only one example of object – every artist chooses what 'lump of stuff' is significant beyond all others and can reveal itself as a whole. This wideness of grasp, this authority, this refusal to be sidetracked, is the mark of creativity.

Is the brain's organization written in stone? Apparently not. It seems you can retrain yourself to grasp wholeness. In the brain, something new is going on; cupboards are being cleared out and heavy furniture dragged around. Neurologically, the traffic on the cortical pathways is changing with a pouring downward of signals absorbing or wiping out old sequences, re-forming, involving and connecting new information and new patterns.

In your work as an artist, these internal disruptions can cause a quantum leap – having seen the whole, you can move past and through the subsets, and subsets of subsets, the nodes and tied strings which interrupt your creativity.

Think of two or three of your favourite artists – try intuitively to identify them by their personal grasp of some otherwise non-evident whole. Proportion, composition, colour range – for each artist's work the characteristic features can be seen as the result of a larger, stranger, personal embracement, one that has dispensed with the clutter and ripened the sight.

Naming the Nameless

'He isn't on anyone's side… and his love for all these things is directed at the nameless.'

Rainer Maria Rilke, on Paul Cézanne

We have been looking at objects, and you may have noticed already that object-making the stuff of the world means naming it. This is how we learned as children – by touching, seeing and gradually learning names for the parts of the world – the parts our culture sees as objects. The most important to us we learned first, and so on and on. We learned to organize the world as we learned to say its names.

Naming

Think of the human body and name some of its parts. Make a quick drawing of a human figure from memory.

Naming the body is almost too easy – head, arm, leg, hand, torso, foot, eyes-nose-and-mouth – we all know the components of the body and how they add up. Every part has a name, and if we study artists' anatomy we can learn more and more parts, and more and more names for them.

The joy of naming

Ever since the animals paraded before Adam, we have enjoyed naming everything in sight. It is our nature to do so. To name is uniquely human. It's one way we structure the world.

But right now, as artists, we need to question how useful these names are. Did you ever walk through the woods and see a plant or hear a bird singing, and feel anxious if you couldn't immediately announce its name? What is this anxiety, and why the sense of relief when the name comes up? Are our minds so structured that we must know the bird's name in order to hear it, to make sense of its song? Does the sound improve? Does the bird need its name in order to sing?

In terms of the brain, the act of attaching the name to the bird validates the fact that that we have remembered and recognized (become-again-cognizant-of) the bird. Now we can settle in comfortably with its invariant representation. We aren't interested in more minute particulars reaching us from the world; these have become unnecessary.

The danger of names

There is security in knowing the names of things, as if in this way we had gained a kind of power over them. It is an old magic. 'I didn't *catch* your name,' we say. It is something to get hold of, and keep. There are drawbacks, however. Naming occurs at the expense of further learning and discrimination.

To name something is gratifying, writes Primo Levi, 'but it is also dangerous: the danger consists in becoming convinced that all is taken care of and that once named, the phenomenon has also been explained'. Now that we have the name, we need not concern ourselves about what its particular nature might be; we believe we know more about it than before. Naming changes our relationship to the previously nameless by giving us a sense of ownership, allowing us a sense of mastery. A name is already a generalization, glued to the invariant.

What has this to do with being an artist? Name-applied-to-object equals invariant representation. To name blinds you to new information and to new ways of assembling the already known. It allows you to use the invariant as ready-made 'knowledge' rather than taking the trouble to look at the particular. Right now we are using the human body as a prime example, to see how its applied names are a means of mentally – and then kinetically – dividing and subdividing it. They prevent us from attending to its unity. A further problem is that the names we have are not always appropriate in terms of form.

Would it be possible to draw the human body – to draw anything – as nameless? To go out there somewhere and locate – and then draw – what has no name at all?

Throw away the lights, the definitions,
And say of what you see in the dark

That it is this or that it is that,
But do not use the rotted names.
(From Wallace Stevens, 'The Man with the Blue Guitar')

The silence between

To render such a familiar object as the human body nameless might seem an impossible task. We could liken it to the naïve idea of seeing 'like a baby', unhindered by knowledge, when in reality our visual system is structured from the start. Yet as we learned when exploring other kinds of visual attention, it's worth trying, if just in order to find out how near we are to the edge of the roof.

> *Use a model or a big mirror. Write on top of your paper NO NAME. Find a couple of named body parts which meet or connect in some way. Now look for the area where they connect, the place where the two names seem to flow and melt into each other, and where neither name really applies.*

You are moving into another kind to attention, removing your focus from the gluey clutch of either of the names, and settling into the *silence between*. You can call this nameless place a *connection* or *transition*, if you still need the comfort of a word.

> *Having found where you want to draw, somewhere between two named parts, draw it any way you like.*

A joint has a name too

The result might be unrecognizable. Maybe you felt you ought not to look for any details, and the only solution was to present a fuzzy mass and hope for the best. Or it is all too sadly identifiable – a lumpy knee, a knobbly, circular elbow – named parts indeed, even though you chose them as being between bigger names like *thigh* and *lower leg*, or between *upper arm* and *lower arm*. A joint usually has a name.

These drawings of 'jointy things' are useful because, if you look more closely, you can discover unnamed connections all around them – if you drew a knee, it is where knee moves into *thigh*, or if you drew an ankle, where *ankle* slides namelessly into *foot*.

Drawing between the names

You may decide at first that there aren't any nameless connections. You could argue that for anyone knowing enough anatomy, every part of the body has a name. Even the word *connection* is a substantive, a thing, a kind of object.

 *Make several more drawings.*

The desire to hang on to names is powerful and it's hard to let them go. One way, at the start, is to announce or write down the names of the two parts you are going to *not* pay attention to. If what I draw has no name, I can at least satisfy my naming-hunger by saying, 'I am drawing between this name and that one.' But your attention needs to change entirely, to let go, to allow you into the actuality and authority of the silence between. Where thumb moves into hand, for example, there is no name because neither *thumb* nor *hand* applies there on.

This need to explain, to name the surrounding forms, will weaken and relinquish its hold. It gets easier to decide where you intend to draw. As for the ordinary, technical means of getting what you see down on the page, remember that you can still use what you learned about mass, and actually draw *through* the form.

 *Try starting with your chalk on its side and establishing where the drawing is going to be. You can*

extend through the connection, speak aloud about
direction as well as its mass.

Directions through

Your first drawings, even when they are right on target, might appear short, lumpy and thing-like. Think about how you can begin to extend more loosely; ask yourself about insertions and meltings-into, the long *directions* that you see.

In drawing direction, in moving back and forth through the nameless area, it's fun to use line. Line suggests the tendons that exist under the skin and are often visible – those parts of the muscle that really are long and thin and flow past the joints. Their direction is *through*, not across, the forms.

How not what

It's fun to draw close up to very definitely named objects. How does, for example, jaw meet ear, and how does ear, from the back, meet head? It is almost guaranteed you have never looked carefully here before. Where fingers connect with the rest of the hand or, even better, where toes join the rest of the foot are new areas of attention. Or you can choose an overlap – to draw, for example, between the nose in three-quarter view and the cheek behind it. Or how one large form lies up against or in front of another.

You might complain that in order to draw between names you do have to draw the named forms, or at least part of them. Of course you do. It is a question of redirecting your attention. No longer are you paying attention to two separate objects with names, but to *how* they connect. It's an enormous help to ask yourself *how* rather than *what* you are drawing. *How* does this named form move into (or connect to, or overlap) this one? The *how* fixes your attention exactly where it should be.

The arrow of attention

Look closely at the drawing on the frontispiece of the book (p. 2). In this very beautiful drawing Michelangelo did a strange thing. Just at the shoulder, on the contour, he made a kind of arrow, or marker (there are actually two on the drawing) – a tiny circle with a thin line extending from it, touching the body with precision. What did he mean?

I believe this is his *arrow of attention*, a visible mark meant to bring his gaze just where he wanted it.

Make some bigger drawings. Draw at least up to life size, or even bigger. Decide first where the connection between the two names is. Be as accurate as you can. Make the broad marks of direction through, from named form to named form. Then, right at the meeting-place, fix your arrow of attention. Like Michelangelo's, it should touch the exact place in between the names, the nameless. This is where your attention must focus. A sloppy arrow of attention pretty much guarantees a sloppy drawing. Can you be accurate? Can you keep your attention there?

There should be room for details. After you have established the direction through, you can break surface and draw the contours, and then surface details, using a sharply sensitive, incision-like line. See how these linear closures punctuate your drawing. Remember that if your attention is on the silence, the details will not intrude, but will enrich whatever you draw.

Not finishing off

'All of Rodin's drawings are completed, even if they are not all finished.' You might still be almost irresistibly tempted to 'just finish off' – for example, draw around the whole of the thumb or finger after you have painstakingly worked through the connection between it and the rest of the hand. The terms 'finishing off' or 'rounding off' tell clearly that your attention has been diverted into the invariants, the gluey names. Yet it's an incomplete kind of diversion – as if you had half an eye on what's out there, and half an eye on the invariant. And it shows.

Nameless life and utter silence

Rilke called Rodin's drawings 'strange documents'. He noted that Rodin, 'keeping his eye constantly on the model, and leaving the paper entirely to his experienced and rapid hand, drew what until then had been neither seen nor recorded... associations of movement that had hitherto been overlooked and unrecognized... A whole new vista filled with nameless life had been discovered; profundities, over which all others had passed with echoing steps, yielded to him their deeps.'

Did you notice that, each time you began, you felt a bit lost and exasperated – 'I can't find any more nameless places, and this is boring anyway' – but that as soon as you made a choice and committed yourself to it, something changed? A special kind of silence settled over this work – the silence of the nameless. When you no longer allow yourself to name, when you begin to look beyond and between the names, you are stepping out into unknown territory. All the hassle about technique and 'how to draw' does not matter – you know how to draw because you know how to see.

What is out there?

It's scary to venture out into the nameless. It takes courage. At times it seems almost impossible. Giacometti said, 'One could spend one's whole life at it without getting anywhere. The shape keeps changing, and it is like dots shifting against a deep, black emptiness: the distance between one nostril and the other is like the Sahara, limitless, featureless, nothing to fasten on to.'

It's OK to be scared. You are not really on your own. Something is out there – everything, the real, true information you are committed to. And what is amazing is how, as you draw, more and more reveals itself. Have you noticed how the 'boring' area you were looking at kept getting more detailed and interesting? This change was not imaginary, but physical – you began to register, consciously, what was unavailable to you at the start. Your retina, through the mechanism of attention, can and does allow more and more information through. This is what is meant by *storms of generosity*. The visual world is astoundingly generous. In a sense, you need not strive. You just have to position your gaze and have the intelligence to step out of the way.

An example

At this time the quality of your drawing may improve quite suddenly, in one leap. Let's take an imaginary example. You decide to draw how the toes meet the foot – not *toes* as such, and not *foot* as such, but the way they are connected. Either you take your shoe and sock off and stretch your foot out (or see it in the mirror for a view of the underside) or you draw from a model. You have often drawn toes and feet, no problem. Yet as you begin to pay attention to the nameless, you find out you have never seen this area properly in your whole life. You start by making some soft grey direction marks, from the ball of the foot into the five toes. It's not too late to draw big, so you extend more across the paper to make a really outsized drawing, giving yourself lots of space. Then, with the grey, smudgy direction established, you carefully draw in your pointed arrow of attention to touch right at the nameless place between the foot and the big toe.

From here on it's new, strange and liberating. Your brain has gone silent. As you continue, even more detail shows itself: what was just an edge turns out to have a kind of shimmery quality; and a crease is more than a line – it has woolliness pressed into it, intensifying its depth and blackness. Tiny details keep appearing. Your arrow – or more arrows, one for each start of a toe – will keep you from getting off target or seeing toes as objects to be finished off. They stay unfinished.

When you are through it's like walking out of an odd kind of deafness. The drawing might look more like a dry-stone wall than a piece of human anatomy. But it is beautiful.

Your drawings of the unnamed connections – with your attention held there in the silence between the names – are often unrecognizable. By now you've made enough of them to understand that they need not be explained. They have an organic truthfulness, and are unusual and exciting graphic works.

They are also examples of how an artist creates using any subject, any material, any theme. Whatever you paint, draw or sculpt, this new decision-making, this regathering and redistribution, this searching out of connections, is at the core of artistic endeavour. It's a new kind of plumping up and shaking down of the visual stuff of the world.

How names make us see

It is not that we must at all costs avoid names. We are human and naming is our business. But when we choose to see only the named parts, we are accessing the invariant representation, holding up a kind of grid that intersects and interferes – a structure that divides the body name by name into preconceived lumps. The fact that a head is called a *head* encourages us – in a way commands us – to see it on its own, and to draw it on its own; and this goes for the other named parts as well. We are using the body as a prime example; later we will see how casual naming can interfere with other themes and subjects, including imagined ones.

Body parts

Most how-to-draw manuals divide the body up into so many 'heads'. The head becomes the measure, imposing itself on the rest of the body, which conveniently squares itself off, like a butcher's diagram of the cuts of beef, along the dotted lines.

Then there is history. We all know Leonardo's Vitruvian Man, drawn standing with limbs outstretched inside a perfect circle. Along with many other studies of human proportion he still seems to bless such a pursuit. Yet he was made for another purpose and is far from accurate. The anthropomorphic canon originated with Plato and Vitruvius and was reinstated in the heady days of the Renaissance, when man was *the measure of all things* and required to represent all proportionality. And if he didn't fit, he was stretched or squeezed until he did. We might speculate, looking at the butcher's diagram, how a human body might be quartered off were it considered edible. It's as much utility as structure which dictates the parts to be named and objectified.

At any rate, the idea of the divided body is reinforced by studying proportion. You are encouraged to see the body as a series of predetermined, joined parts, glued together but essentially parts. You may even own a lay figure – one of those wooden, jointed dolls sold in art stores. Even when the attempt is to get an idea of wholeness, perceptual glue is still applied at the old joining-places.

Certainly the head is a head. But to name it demands that we give it boundaries, concentrate on it exclusively. In drawing a head we work exclusively with head-ness, our attention rigidly confined by its invariant name. The place where *head-ness* moves into neck-ness has no name, and so we don't bother to see it.

Rodin's biographer Bourdelle has him say, in answer to a complaint about two 'headless' statues: 'The heads of those bodies? What are you talking about?… You have understood nothing! The question is nonsense. Why, in my art the head is everywhere!' When you draw by extending, you follow an outpouring of energy from an *interior source*. Bourdelle again: *'Make all of your parts live!* If you know where the living source of forms is found, the gaze that follows the warp of your work will recognize the shock of palpitation coming from those interior sources and thought will create the absent parts by the vitality of the parts that are active.' This is a good example of the difference between 'finished off' and 'completed'; the statues were not 'finished off,' yet because of their internal unity they were complete.

When you drew by extending the figure's mass, moved with your chalk out of the centre and up into the head, you might have managed to stay the top-down cascade, and inhibit the head-invariant and its insistence on itself as a separate object. But it was difficult. We know that the head-invariant is powerfully entrenched, with part of the cortex (the *fusiform gyrus*) dedicated to the recognition of faces and facial expression. Consider the art of almost all cultures – the head is the central image. As you drew, did you notice the seductive pull, the numinosity of the head whenever you came near? Is this the event horizon where, once you get close, you get sucked in and there's no way back? Later we will be exploring this dominant image and its meaning for us as artists. Right now we are into trying to move into the unknown, see what is not named, not objectified.

Hopping from name to name

Names grab and direct our attention in a jerky, divisive manner, and it's almost inevitable that we 'read' the model in the old rote ways, from name to name.

Look at the drawing you made at the beginning of the chapter (p. 127) while naming the parts of the body. Look for any breaks in the line.

A break in the line signals a break in your attention. It looks as if you took a breath and hopped over. If you were to wander around a life drawing class, you would see example after example of this kind of drawing, each part drawn and each connection visibly missing. Sometimes it is the faintest of breaks, a catch of breath, which serves to isolate the one named part from the next. The breaks are predictable – between head and neck, limbs and hands or feet. Sometimes a joint itself is isolated – a knee or elbow. Breasts are drawn on their own. It's fun to check the joints or nodes, because they so obviously reveal the stop-and-start-again mechanism – chalk or pencil or brush literally lifted from the page. Now that you have learned how the mind categorizes, you know the reason.

If you are one of the many who still tend to 'take a breath' between drawing each ordinary named part, and hop over, you'll see it on the evidence of your drawings.

If so, try a drastic, temporary solution – behavioural psychology. The idea is that the behaviour, or symptom, is forcibly stopped first; later one can get on with treating the reasons behind it. Make a drawing of a figure while not lifting the chalk off the paper at all. Hold your drawing hand down with the other one if necessary.

Natural or cultural discontinuities?

We have noticed how, as each named form is drawn, the line peters out, takes a breath, and resumes. The trouble is that the names, the invariants, have perceptual borders which may not form 'natural discontinuities'. As with the butcher's diagram, names are culturally as much as naturally imposed. There may be other discontinuities, exciting ones as yet undiscovered, and your attention should be open to see them.

Mode and costume

Oddly enough the world of fashion has a bearing here. Dress and the history of dress, costume and culture, the huge modern fashion industry – isn't it all just about redividing the human body? Within certain practical restrictions (you have to be able to keep warm, and to move), almost anything goes in the ways the body is sectioned off and subdivided by clothing. And there's a certain buzz and excitement with a really different style. Fashion is an endless, changing arena, one we are affected by even if we consider it unworthy of our interest. Fashion boils down to finding new discontinuities – ways of dividing and seeing the human body anew. From the height of the waistline to the length of soccer shorts and swimming costumes, fashion is forever in change, yet pretty much instantly recognizable by date and culture.

> *Think of the changes in fashion you have experienced in your own lifetime. How did you dress as a child compared to how children dress today? What about how older people dress? Think if you like about special apparel – party dresses, sports clothes, school wear, boots and shoes. Does the change not usually involve the division of some body part in a different way – skirt length, sleeves, and so on? Cast your mind back across time and think how much you know about what's called style. Think of your parents' dress, their parents', Victorian times, further back; let your imagination roam away into the past.*

Present mode seems chaotic, borrowing indiscriminately from all over. Immersed in the culture, you can't yet see an overall pattern. It's like contemporary slang – language is in flux, and some new words will enter it for good, some will disappear. Meanwhile, without thinking about it, you are absorbing and memorizing and compartmentalizing, and in twenty years you'll be able to date today's fashion, like today's slang, to within half a decade.

This play with clothing is creative play. It involves varieties of texture and pigment as well as the renaming and reshaping of form. It can teach us that the name, the object, is never sacrosanct, that change and regrouping, realigning and recategorizing, is a continuing human activity indulged in because it's good fun – in other words, creative.

Unjamming the scan paths

Remember learning about scan paths and how they are returned to again and again, whenever an object is recognized? We draw the way we do because our scanning apparatus is jammed, persisting in old patterns that superficially explore each recognized, named object (like *head*) before nipping along to the next. It is jammed because of drawing habits which, in turn, are the direct result of the name, the top-down interference of the invariant. We *recognize* the body as a series of named parts.

In learning to see, we chose to bring order to the visible world, and in doing so we chose, albeit unconsciously, the precise direction and length of each saccade. That path is predicted before we embark on it. Can the scan paths be unjammed? Can we make other, more useful choices? Changing those patterns, even taking conscious responsibility for changing them, may be possible.

Look back at the drawings you have made, and consider them in terms of unjamming the scanning mechanism.

As soon as you began working with the space close to the object, and certainly later in the building up of mass from the perceived core, your habitual scan paths were definitely disrupted: you could not use your ordinary, sequential ways of seeing. Now, moving in the nameless places between the parts, you are again denying yourself access to familiar paths. You have not been *recognizing*, but instead training yourself to create new paths, describing different assemblies.

The difficulties you encountered, the slipping back into the parts, can be explained in the light of your natural preference for established paths, the invariant representations.

Being allowed to name

We love to name, and it feels uncomfortable to be denied this natural activity. Yet the names we have are not always pertinent in terms of perceived form. The *perceptive glue* is applied in the wrong places. It may be possible to glue the body more appropriately, to be allowed to give it new, more suitable names.

> *Choose a place where one part meets or*
> *melts into another. As you draw it, name it. Try*
> *to find a name that suits it, something quite*
> *new. Perhaps now that you know you are*
> *drawing the* qlff, *you will allow yourself to see it*
> *more clearly.*

This is the mysterious human body, and its names are not born to it; they have been imposed and there is no reason to accept them, or their divisions, for absolutes. They are inventions, just like the ones on the butcher's diagram – the ox with its shank and rib and loin and so on. And, for that matter, like the diagrams in books about how to draw the model. Perhaps on some Pacific island the people really call this beautiful turn of the neck into the chin the flala, and celebrate it in their songs. Perhaps, there between the shoulder blade and the shoulder, that dusky dip has a secret name waiting for you to speak it as you draw.

Name plus object

Does naming an object actually change our perception of it? Recent research has been able to pinpoint just where in the brain we recognize and respond to objects, and where we respond to their names. Images and words engage different brain circuits, even hemispheres, which can – but do not always – 'talk to' each other. For example, a name can activate the image of an object, but the image does not always activate the name. Memory seems to be enhanced by consciously concentrating on both the visible object and the name for it, and this finding does feel intuitively right – think about how you yourself decide to remember something. 'Now I am putting the *keys* here, on the *hall shelf*. I have to remember that' (with emphasis on the word *keys* and the visible image of placing them).

Location is hemispheric: words on their own activate cells in the left frontal lobe, and objects you have no name for activate a region on the right. Naming the object activates both sides, and this global use of the brain, plus the attentional act of telling ourselves to remember, has been proven to enhance memory. It has also been shown recently that the brain gets excited and intrigued when ordinary colours are given funny new names, though neurologists need only have asked marketing and sales (in anything from cars to home decoration) about that – it's something they have understood and exploited for decades.

Remember when you drew the bays and promontories, hills and hollows – the wash of space against the object in the centre? Already your attention was directed away from the ordinary parts and their labels, as unexpected words brought new areas to your attention.

The work of the poet is essentially the renaming and reordering of 'ordinary' reality. Through extraordinary namings and stunning analogies, we may suddenly apprehend the truth – what Robert Lowell called 'any clear thing that blinds us with surprise.' In 'Fishnet', he uses this lowly image for his lifelong craft, and concludes in affirmation.

> *The line must terminate.*
> *Yet my heart rises, I know I've gladdened a lifetime*
> *knotting, undoing a fishnet of tarred rope;*
> *the net will hang on the wall when the fish are eaten,*
> *nailed like illegible bronze on the futureless future.*

You can experience for yourself how attention, redirected through unfamiliar words, can result in art. Keep in mind the passage about Giacometti's space. Now, through names which guide the eyes, you will look at space in a new way. And at the same time you will be drawing your beloved surface detail.

The sack of space

Remember when you were looking at space close to the object, drawing the small embracement, how space was shaped and enclosed? Now try giving it a name.

⟜⊘ *Look towards yourself in the mirror and sit hunched forward. Or, with a model, choose a pose in which she hunches forward. See whether you can rename the space in front of the figure as a sack, filled with space, held between the arms, under the chin or face, and above the thighs. Can you see this area renamed? Write SACK OF SPACE on the paper, and make a drawing.*

All you can actually see of it is, of course, where it makes contact with the body – along the inner sides of hands, arms and shoulders, the convex curve of the torso hollowed to receive it, the upper surface of the thighs.

If your attention is on that space, it will contain details of the body embracing it, and no more. Like your drawings of the nameless connections, it will be concentrated there. No extenuating details, like the top of the head, or the outside of the arms, will appear.   •

⟜⊘ *Look at the drawing and check that it contains only the confines of the sack of space. If you have drawn more (such as the outside of the figure), it's either because you never saw and isolated that inner embracement, or because you couldn't resist, after you had drawn it, your desire to 'finish off'. Make another drawing, again naming it, this time using an arrow of attention, to keep yourself focused on the sack.*

Almost all poses contain some embracements of space you can look for, right down to the hollow of the hand. Naming and looking for these enclosures, large or small, frees you to draw in new and more truthful ways. In many poses, like this one, you can check out the closeness of the face to the hands or knees. It is as though they were having a conversation. In many a drawing the head is drawn on its own, rigidly upright as if on a string, pulled away from what it actually broods over. It is fun to take the space into account and to ask, 'Are they talking to one other?'

A nursing mother

Here is a good example of how and how not to proceed – a study of a mother nursing her baby. If you draw sequentially, after the names, you'll begin with the two heads, even if it's just to sketch them in lightly to 'guide' you. Your attention isolates them, even though you may have taken a second or two to check the relative size and location of each.

Suppose you began instead with the conversation, the connection, the silence between? Your attention from the start would be on what is happening between the two heads. If you concentrated on, and drew this area accurately, no more would be needed – certainly no 'finishing off' of the top or back of the mother's head and shoulders.

There seems to be no halfway solution. Tentative sketching-in of the heads and then attention to the space does not work. You can almost follow the doomed process in imagination; it would go something like this: 'Let me see. This big head goes here, and this little head goes here. Now I have established that and I can continue with more careful drawing of each and, oh yes, fill in whatever is in between and around them.'

Such a drawing would be inevitably unsatisfactory in boring, predictable ways. Any observer would scan it as you did, as two unrelated objects. This is supposed to represent a unique relationship, an embracement, a conversation. The space between is what matters, and ought to absorb your impeccable attention. You must choose intelligently, right at the beginning. Choose to see with Rodin's ripeness of sight. Choose to think largely and wordlessly. Choose to enter the unknown. Great artists do not necessarily draw better than lesser ones; they choose better.

The cave

Another useful name which can change and enhance your perception is *cave* – you may use it for any shape your gaze can enter and wander around in.

Sit so that you can see into the cave. There is definitely a roof, side walls, back wall and floor. There may even be several entrances.

Use a mirror or a model, and another hunched-forward pose. Begin by looking, and attending to the embracement as if seeing into a cave. Think of the walls pressing in and the roof pressing down (the word concavity has the same source as the word cave – it's as if a Stone Age man had lit a fire and the smoke was filling up a cave and all its crannies. You can even start by indicating the smoke). Then go right into details.

Again, nothing extraneous should be recorded about this being part of an object with another name, because right now it is not: the only part that is of interest is the cave, made visible by its borders.

The roof of the cave may be the lowered face, or

the underside of an arm stretched across drawn-up knees, the sides of the cave formed by the inner sides of the thighs, and the back of the cave, curving away between them, comprising the torso with its surface details. Seen as a 'pose', it looks pretty difficult – so many named parts to be assembled, problems of proportion, tone, foreshortening and so on. But if you are looking into a cave, you can forget all that – you will be all right. Draw big. Give yourself space to be accurate in.

It is in order to think rock face, stalactites and stalagmites. The facial profile, the inner side of wrist and hand, are now nothing but nameless rock, pushing out into the cave-space in very particular, jagged ways. As you work on the cave walls your eye should be crossing the area between them from side to side, and grasping the cave's exact width, depth and height, assessing how the walls talk to each other across space.

Again, the word *talk* is better than the word *relate* – it's a communication you can listen to and almost hear, a sort of charge or shimmering that connects the edges, aural and even tactile, like the bouncing off of radar, letting you experience the exact shape and enabling you to draw it accurately.

New names, larger silences

Drawing the nameless body works very well on small transitions, but what about the larger view? Names are all over the place. Again, it is a matter of choice and attention.

It is possible to rename, and so perceive, larger areas. With the human body as an example, you can discover important new assemblies embracing the old nodes and ignoring the old discontinuities, and be ready to name them, to be Adams-and-Eves in Eden.

Mirror cells

How does the body move and function? A good way to find out is to combine watching the model and trying things out for yourself.

Drawing the model has a special attraction, and taking on the same pose in order to understand it is an ordinary part of life drawing. There are reasons. It's been discovered recently that the brain has a sophisticated circuitry which resonates to what other people are doing. Called the *mirror neuron mechanism*, its origins are thought to precede and underlie language, which has evolved from gestures. Pointing was once grasping; we open our lips slightly wider (try it) when looking at a bigger image; we mimic facial expressions, and feel what others feel when they produce them. Complex assemblies of *mirror cells* are automatically stimulated by actions we observe – or even predict. There is even an area for processing mental images of action, reached by a path that separates off early in the visual process. Imitation, empathy, mind reading – perhaps mass hysteria and the behaviour of crowds – have a neurological explanation.

Now, as you watch the model, you activate a template based on your own movements: your mirror cells are responding.

If you can look at a model, watch how her shoulder blade swivels upward when she lifts her arm; then feel your own. Feel the whole upper area of your torso partaking in the movement. Lift your arm and swing it around. How much gets in on the movement? Watch, and feel, how the whole shoulder area is involved, as well as chest muscles and shoulder blade, all joining in the rotation.

It's pretty well impossible to move your arm on its own. The pectorals arise from collarbone and breast-bone and spread their strong fibres right across the chest and down into the arm, and you can feel them pulling as you move your arms back. Muscles are not squared off, stopping and starting at the joints. They are continuous from their origins into their insertions. Look for this aspect. Many have long tendons which ignore and flow past the joints. The extensors of your wrist, for example, originate above the elbow. The extensors of fingers or toes are rope-like, stretching high into arm or leg. The strap-like *sartorius*, longest muscle in the body, arises from the high anterior crest of the pelvis, and spirals all the way down and around behind the knee to insert into the *tibia* in the lower leg.

Muscles are like capes, wraps or slings, covering and binding ordinary bony divisions. The body is bandaged with these smooth cloths of fossa and sinew, with branching and rejoining tributaries, ribbons and threads. Maybe the body-builder's desire for 'definition' is really the brain's insatiable desire to co-opt even these forms into hard-edged lumps? On the other hand, what is the grace we look for in dance? We love to watch the 'ease' of dance – that cooperative, unified flow. A more useful artist's anatomy would address the muscles, rather than the skeleton, as the measure of the functioning body.

Stretch your fingers, and feel the long connections. Swing your arm again and test how much of your body is involved.

Experiment with what we call the leg, and see whether you can decide where it leaves off. When you swing your leg, your whole lower torso is in motion. Or look at the model as she stretches her leg; you cannot see any division between leg and torso. There is none – it is your brain supplying the node and the separation.

Origins and insertions

So begin to pay attention to *origins and insertions*, rather than to the named parts which these muscles show up on and operate. The muscles span the areas of articulation and are not stopped by joints. And this wider view applies to any structure you want to understand, not just the human body. Suppose you were to make a descriptive drawing of a bridge. It would be a poor representation if it were not shown to be attached firmly into both banks.

Finally, stretch your neck back, and watch someone else do so. Feel how the thrust comes from far down inside the chest. Sense, then see, a solid, deeply rooted form rising out of the torso and reaching right on up into the head.

How can the names chest, neck, head describe this single mass?

Body work

There are many systems for improving or correcting some

aspect of the body. Whether you dance, train, or practise yoga, you'll know about them. Several, like the Alexander Technique and Pilates, concern themselves with just this idea of more coherence and fluidity. They still, for practicality's sake, use the customary divisions and names, and I am convinced that this makes for a more uphill battle than it would otherwise be. The only method I've come across which takes that leap into the nameless is Feldenkrais. It is based not on the muscular but on the nervous system. It is extremely slow: you start with repetitive, small, isolated movements, which are gradually extended until the whole body partakes, and actually teaches *itself* new (and more appropriate) ways of moving. Many musicians swear by it. I am continually surprised. The unified source of energy and movement I'd been talking about all these years can be felt as well as seen, experienced as well as perceived. *Feldenkrais* for Artists should be on offer as a course – maybe it will some day.

Meaningful new names

Is it possible to find more useful, appropriate names that encompass the reality of the body?

A new name can be meaningful, not just nonsense sounds. A new name gives your attention something to hold on to in the widest possible, pan-hemispheric, global way, so you do not get seduced back into the old names and divisions. For example, you could call the three big areas described above **torm**, **lumb** and **streck**.

Torm is how your arm moves out of the torso. It comprises that area of the torso which partakes in its movement, on through the shoulder and out towards (but not including) the elbow.

Lumb is how the leg moves out of the torso. It comprises that area of the torso which partakes in its movement, on through the hip and down towards (but not including) the knee.

Streck is how the head moves out of the torso. It comprises that area of the torso which partakes in its movement, on through the neck and deep into the head (but not finishing off the top of it).

Stand (before the mirror) or have a model stand with weight on one foot and the opposing arm lifted (perhaps resting on the head), the other arm somewhere out of the way. Think about how one leg – and how the raised arm – is extending out of deep roots within the torso. If you want to use the new names for these large areas, call them torm *and* lumb, *and choose to look at one of them, then the other.*

The direction of mass

These new forms are elongated, so as to see – and draw – direction from the start.

Make two beginning drawings – one of the torm *(how the raised arm originates and extends from deep in the torso) and one of the* lumb *(how the leg originates and extends from deep inside the torso).*

Pay attention to the long, stretching verticals. You could use chalk laid on its side or long lines of direction. These marks are like the muscles, flowing through joints, connecting. Allow yourself to draw big – right up to size if you can.

How much to draw?

Your choice of how much to draw depends on your motoric
sense as well as on vision. Your body knows and can tell you
what is involved. Suppose you wanted to draw a line with felt
pen around the *torm*. You'd probably draw under (to include)
the entire shoulder blade and right over to the spine, and
at the front, the whole chest area to the sternum, and some of
the neck as well – and then, to limit its extension into the arm,
make a ring about halfway to the elbow. These lines do not
record true edges, like the edges of form, but perceptual ones.
In reality the area of the *torm* fades gradually as involvement
diminishes, and your drawing will show this, getting lighter
and more tenuous as the name ceases to apply.

Stand in the pose and think torm, *and extend your
attention out into the far reaches. Make a few small
movements and adjustments, test sensation from the
inside, pick up the signal. Think about the flow. All the
information you need is available to you.*

In drawing the torm, *stay first with the sweeping
directions that bring you out of the chest or back, and
through the shoulder into the arm. Then come to the
surface. Note that on the inside, where arm and shoulder
are close to the head, the form is squashed and has broken
contours that overlap each other. Choose one of these
overlapped contours, and pay careful attention to exactly
how and where it emerges. This is definitely a place where
you do not want to 'hold your breath' and jump a bit.
Choose precisely where the edge emerges and begin right
there, in exact touch with the contour it emerges from.*

Then, with your 'drifting' line, follow the long outer

contours. See how different in quality the compressed inner edges are from these long, simple outside ones. Maybe your line itself is heavier and harsher where the contours are squashed, finer and more flowing where the form is extended.

Resist the invariant

It is hard to leave well alone, and if you are drawing the model you might feel you 'just have to finish off' the breast so tantalizingly close to what you are supposed to be looking at – after all, it is there, partaking in the sweep of chest into shoulder. Or, as the lines of direction move out along the arm, you can't resist just adding the elbow or even rounding off the fingers.

The object with its name sucks away attention into itself. Breast-as-object does not exist in the *torm*. Here's the difference – if you focus your attention impeccably on the new, large name and what it means, you will draw not a *what*, a thing, for example a breast-object, but instead, *how* the breast partakes subtly in the upward flow of the *torm*. And the difference will be apparent in your drawing.

Yes, these big, comprehensive areas do cross the domains of old names (like *breast, shoulder, hip*) which lie in wait like underwater logs or outcroppings, ready to snag your attention. Take care to float through, carried by the current of the large, long direction.

The *lumb*

We seem extraordinarily hung up on the rear. If you draw the *lumb* from the back, you have to navigate this perceptual boulder, and it's far from easy. The horizontal crease seems to be a natural division, a ready-made line separating the hip (and torso) from the leg. This is a prime example of how the brain wants to create and separate objects. Many drawings founder here, ending up as a globe-shaped object stuck on top of a cylindrical one, with a deeply gouged dividing line between. It's hard to accept that the brain has actually taught us to see and separate one form into two distinct objects, and encourages us to enforce this imaginary separation.

If you have a chance, watch the model swing her leg and move slowly around, shifting her weight from the one foot to the other. Or try these movements yourself.

Look first at two objects – the torso and the leg. Get even more specific and look at the buttock and the thigh. These are all too easy to locate and isolate as shapes or lumps of stuff – a globe and a cylinder.

Now make a shift of attention and look at the lumb. *This is harder. Watch as the model moves, how the long form (through the hip into the thigh) gets longer when she stretches her leg or takes the weight off it. Squint, and check out the values and what they are telling you about form. Chances are the tone is darkest along the side and the cross-shadow under the buttock is practically non-existent. You may have invented it. It may indistinctly come and go. Its significance has made you exaggerate it in terms of tone. Look instead for the long, nameless vertical shadows on the length of the hip and thigh. Keep these in mind as you squint at the cross-crease under the buttock and realize how visually irrelevant it is.*

It's not a case of drawing differently from what you see, but rather, of drawing what is actually there before it gets separated off and loaded with meaning in the brain. If you've seen and drawn a flowing, unified *lumb*, it's fine to draw the cross-crease where you happen to see it, carefully, as an interesting surface detail. It's the mind's determination to separate hip from leg which has drenched it with unearned importance and caused the perceptual glitch.

Women's bathing suits are a good example of how fashion can help us see. Remember those once universal cross-the-crease hems? They came to be regarded as quaint, but there are signs they are returning to favour. The present style while it lasts is good for teaching us to see the *lumb*, with the whole hip area exposed to flow pretty much seamlessly into the thigh.

More arrows of attention

Even in these large drawings, making an arrow of attention is useful. Even here the invariants and their names can grab your attention back into the separate participating forms.

Check the drawings and place the arrow, and see whether you have looked hardest there, where it's neither arm nor shoulder, thigh nor hip. This is where you have to be most exact. In the case of getting past the rears, an arrow of attention at the contour may be all that is needed.

Through into the head (the *streck*)

The final and most difficult renaming concerns the head – or rather, how it extends from the body. We can call this area the *streck*.

⟜◯ *Try lying down, with your head hanging even
further down over the edge of bed or sofa. You can't draw
this in a mirror, unless you are some sort of contortionist,
but it is educational to experience it. Your chest is higher
than your head and your throat area is laid open.*

*A model might agree to take this pose so you can see it,
preferably from eye level – best if she lies on a table. Look
at it from the side or from the head end. Feel or observe
the long, curved, flow through the chest and down through
the throat into the head.*

This pose is not about breasts or shoulders or head, perceived
lumps of stuff basking on their own with their own beguiling
names. It is definitely not about 'how to draw a neck'. The
word *streck* describes an area and an action – it tells *how* the
head extends from its roots deep in the torso. Anyone who has
tried the pose can describe, from what it feels like, how much
it encompasses.

⟜◯ *Try the pose again and note where you actually
feel the* streck. *What muscles in the chest and neck
are involved? How about your shoulders, your jaw
and face? Think negatively – what isn't? The top of
your head is out of range. The intensity of the* streck
*(where you might place the arrow of attention) is
inside, somewhere in the throat, and its direction is
through, in one arching curve. Follow it in sensation
as if your attentive imagination were being borne
along by a current – from the pull of the muscles
below the rib cage, up over the chest, down into the
neck, on towards the back of the neck and down,*

almost vertically now as if over a waterfall, to somewhere inside the head.

Chin – a sharp boulder in the stream

The jaw, with its component the chin, is a real, visible snag in the flow. If you look directly at any head, *chin* makes a natural boundary. If you see the pose at eye level, the chin juts up and seems to demand prior attention. It is difficult to 'place' and you have to ask yourself, what is the highest form in this pose? And even so, against the visible evidence, you might still opt for the chin.

If you have a chance to draw this pose, write NO CHIN on top of the page before you start drawing. If you are drawing an upright pose (as in a mirror) write NO CHIN anyway.

Like the trunk of a tree

Because the head is involved, even seeing the *streck* as an object is very difficult. A head will always want to be on its own, to lift itself up and separate itself off from the body

Unless you have access to a model you can't draw this particular, difficult pose. But you can draw the *streck* anyway, using a mirror. You can learn to see it. It is there whatever the pose, though the unfamiliar, reclining position makes it more evident. If you are using a mirror, your challenge is even greater. You'll be fighting, not just against the invariant download of any old head, but against the most tenacious one of all – the upright head. Later we'll be exploring exactly why the head in this 'ordinary' upright position makes such special demands.

Look for a moment and allow your sight to mature so that you see the streck *like a solid tree-trunk with its deep, grasping roots in the torso. See its movement into the head in one unbroken form – a curved, cylindrical trunk. Draw first – using flowing, soft grey marks – the whole general direction of the* streck. *Don't break the flow by lifting your chalk. You are teaching yourself the* streck's *continuous flow. In the pose, this will be a smooth curve up through the chest (highest) and down into the head (almost vertical). In any pose, it will follow through from chest into head, and peter out. There will be no sketchy outlines – certainly not of the head.*

Mark an arrow of attention where you sense the streck *is at its most tense and intense.*

Taking pains

This is a working drawing and the difficulties you encounter are not caused by lack of talent or ability, but by the interference of the invariant representations. In one sense it should be 'easier' to draw the unfamiliar, because you're forced to go outside and get the information. But every sortie costs. Nothing appears where it ought and the old signposts are gone or disallowed (NO CHIN). Even so, the invariants keep loading down, loading down, and every stroke you make has to be struggled for. 'You know', says the invariant, 'that the head is up, not way down there.' Or 'You know the ear can't possibly be upside down.' The voice of the invariant is like a small devil sitting on your shoulder, carrying on incessantly with all kinds of useful (useless) advice. You have to stand up to it as the drawing progresses.

Your page may get into such a mess you want to begin again. Maybe you made a big mistake at the start and now there's no room for the head. The ear is misplaced (though you might have been smart enough to draw the areas around it to get it right).

When you run into difficulties, don't quit and restart; if you need more paper just tape another sheet alongside. If you misjudged completely, and the whole thing has turned out flat, blacken out or erase or paste paper over the affected area. Worry at it, argue with it, pause and regroup, allow yourself (or force yourself) to make the big, necessary changes.

Perseverance is the mark of the artist. Genius has been called 'the infinite capacity for taking pains'. This is a painful drawing. It will also be a beautiful drawing if you manage to complete it.

Face

Drawing the *streck* is accomplished, for better or for worse. Here is your chance to continue into more unknown territory.

If you are lucky enough to have convinced a model to stay in this uncomfortable pose, and so have time to work on the face, do so. Draw in the same way (continuing to avoid the chin). Betty Edwards introduced the idea of copying line drawings of upside-down faces; this has become a common exercise and you may have tried it. The upside-down face you are looking at now is real, and here, even more evidently, the same experiential

namelessness applies. You have no idea what is going on.
Draw it anyway. Bypass the features; you can't use your
knowledge to place them (witness your having to move the
ear several times already). Instead, pay particular attention
to tone – pieces of nameless shadow – and abstract
patches. There is no 'jaw line' but instead, a beautifully
strange, gritty, nameless desert, Giacometti's Sahara, that
you have never explored before. The hair is a big weighty
mass and falling vertically. Use it to drag the head down
even further.

If you are drawing the upright face in a mirror, try this:
don't draw the features at all. It helps to write on the
drawing NO EYES, NO NOSE, NO MOUTH, NO EARS.
Draw everything else as carefully as you possibly can. (You
are of course able to inch in close to the features.) By
drawing this way you will be forced into the nameless,
where there are no invariants to help (hinder) you.

When the drawing is completed, carefully add the chin
where it belongs. If you have drawn the model, turn the
drawing right around, upside down. Hang it upside down.
Don't correct it.

These drawings, looked at upside down (but perceptually
upside right), are like angels or swimmers or figureheads.
They have enormous power. With no control over likeness,
you may have a great likeness or something totally alien, but
the strangeness of the image is guaranteed to be arresting.
The expression, which you could not read and which you had
no conscious say in, is mindful, inward, with an authority
almost amounting to arrogance. You have no idea where such
an expression came from, or how you were capable of

creating it. You have made a drawing as close as you will ever get to what is really out there, probably full of messy mistakes and overdrawing, but almost uncontaminated by your entrenched knowledge, those invariant representations in your brain.

Reading faces

The *fusiform gyrus* is set aside for faces and facial recognition, and in there, locked into the structure and function of its dedicated cells, is a kind of template of the upright human face. As we have seen, this configuration is innate; infants respond to it from birth. It need not even be made up of features – the surrealist painting by Arcimboldo with vegetables for features will do – if the general eye-eye-nose-mouth relationship is there and upright. Once I watched a bright-two-year-old drawing at a table. He announced that he would draw 'a fish coming out of the water', and made the horizon line – and then drew the fish emerging – on its nearer side. After seeing this I'd guess that a flat image, until the child learns better, can be read as up in both directions. It's logical, and children often crawl around drawings they are working at on the floor. I don't know if it has ever been tested. I often end up on the floor myself, and have tried drawing the model 'as if' the flat paper represented a vertical tipped away from me, which did not improve the results and caused my trained brain a lot of discomfort.

The Danes have an action nursery rhyme that goes:
Punktum, punktum komma, strej
Sådan tegnes Nicolai.
(Dot, dot, comma, line,
That's how Nicolai is drawn.)

And no more is needed to evince the upright-face response.

You 'find faces' in clouds and in the textured bark of trees. You do it because you can't help it; it's pleasurable, a kind of play. Visual psychologists call it *pareidolia* – the brain's ability to create meaningful patterns out of random ones, and it's almost always a human face – for example the Man in the Moon, the 'face' of the stone formation on Mars, the features of Jesus which miraculously appeared on a wall in Ghana. Random expressions, which are completely self-created, surprise and delight, like the Man in the Moon who looks anxiously back over a nonexistent shoulder.

We recognize an upright face, and a host of recognized upright faces, not piecemeal, object by object, but all at once, holistically. This happens very fast, in under one-fifth of a second, and very early in the sequence of the visual process.

Because faces are so similar, and so significant, it isn't surprising to find that the brain dedicates a whole area to them. But recently even more has been discovered – that not only the face, but other objects of 'extreme interest' are also recognized in the *fusiform gyrus*. Given extreme interest, we train ourselves to process other objects there. The examples in the literature are cars (apparently the car fancier's *fusiform gyrus* lights up whenever he recognizes various makes) and what the visual psychologists call 'gimbles' – nameless images which subjects were told to remember, and which were shown to them over and over. Eventually, the reappearance of a gimble fired up the *fusiform gyrus*. (New gimbles left it predictably cold.) The subjects were university students, and their extreme interest must have been the pay for taking part in the experiment.

For you as an artist, this means you can access one of the most sophisticated, complex and fast-acting neural circuits of the visual brain – whenever you train yourself diligently, through repetition, to recognize a category of objects in great detail. 'Extreme interest' means paying attention, which is not a problem for an artist already obsessed by a creative project.

Renaming the whole

We have found new names, *torm*, *lumb* and *streck*, to better describe the large continuities of the body. Would it be possible to rename the whole figure?

Look at a plant or a tree. Can you look at this one object, extending from roots outwards and upwards, as a unity?

As trees, walking

It's easier to see a tree as a whole than to see a figure, though when you look at (or draw or paint) some plants – in particular flowers – you might get caught up in object-parts and lose the continuity and wholeness. You probably noticed how your big drawings of *torm* and *lumb* resembled trees. Keep the image as a new name for the human form. In the biblical story, the blind man whose sight was restored said, 'I see men as trees, walking.'

With your new understanding of, and new names for, the larger areas of the body, seeing the figure as a whole has to be easier. You have already made drawings by massing the figure from the core and extending outwards to the boundaries, swimming past the old divisions, training ripeness of sight. From now on this should gradually become more intuitive. You will not have to say everything aloud – your beginnings may be tentative and sketchy (you have to start somewhere, after all) but no longer will they be those guessed-at boundary-lines around a head or other parts. You will start by saying something, even if it is only in a whisper, about source and unity. And if you draw in line, your drawings will still, in Rodin's words, arise from the place where 'the living source of forms is found,' and anyone who sees them will 'recognize the shock of palpitation coming from those interior sources.'

Renaming the world

Renaming the world is the work of the artist.

Take a walk and practise renaming. Bits and pieces of the visual array can be rearranged in almost infinite ways. And reunified. Try looking, for example, at shadowiness, or brightness; look into the sky as a great overturned bowl with its ragged, patterned brim of trees and housetops. Look for the sudden plunge of a side street, or a shop – a cavern. Look how, and feel, trees and parked vehicles loom and recede in a kind of dance as you go by.

This is the way artists see, choosing large embracements and different simplicities, inviting and entering new silences as they reconstruct and rename the visible world.

Colour, for a change

It's refreshing to work in colour after a long period of using monochrome, or any time when your energy is low. With the Rorschach ink-blot series, the psychologists look for colour shock when a coloured card is presented after a series of monochrome ones. An open reaction, positive or negative, or even a long, puzzled pause, can signify anything from 'repression of affect' to 'masked sexual response', adding to the layman's suspicion that no matter what you answer you're in for it.

Colour shock has been exploited by movie-makers ever since Dorothy and Toto stepped out of brownish Kansas into multicoloured Oz. In general it is pleasurable – you enjoy a sunny day after bad weather, and go into rose gardens in the spring, and every fall in the northeastern USA you can check out the foliage reports on TV to find out where to drive for the most brilliant colours. In the studio, after working in monochrome for hours or days, the sudden chance to play with colour has a real impact.

Root out some short pieces of coloured chalk or crayon. For your subject, you can use a plant, one with a visible stem. If you have a chance now or later, use a model, standing in the centre of the room. (In a class, everyone can join in, each with one colour and moving around to every drawing in turn.) Choose a very simple standing pose – weight resting on one foot, arms resting on the head – but with the torso twisted to give it tension.

Set up for at least six drawings round the room and use one colour all the way round; then continue with another colour, each time using it throughout, on each drawing in turn. Starting with the first colour, lay your chalk on its side and just establish the source or core, recording one mark of direction within the twisted torso or stem.

In drawing a plant or tree your natural inclination would be to draw upwards, following the growth and expanding smoothly from stem into branches. Use this inclination with the model as well. Feel her twist. Look first, and allow your sight to ripen, apprehending the source of the pose. Make one short, upward-moving mark to describe it. Then move to the next paper (this is a new view, so take time again to allow your sight to ripen) and again draw only the source or core. Make a complete round.

On your next round, with a new colour, begin to extend from the source in each drawing. With the model, choose to move from the core up into the neck/head, then on the next round from the core out into an arm (towards the elbow, and again for the other arm.) Then extend from the core downwards into one thigh, and on the next round into the other.

Remember the flow

Your understanding of the unified flow through the connections pays off here. In drawing the plant, you moved smoothly from the stem up into the branches. With the model you know better than to 'finish off' distal parts or encircle the head. There is no need to go even as far as elbows or knees, or to make boundaries for the head, and of course no need to be snagged by objects like chin, breasts or buttocks. Your drawings reach from the source in a single, unbroken mark.

Breaking surface

Begin your new mark at the source every time, moving in a seamless extension, allowing it to become longer and longer.

On this round, begin to come to the surface, still from the core. For example, beginning with the core, move down towards the thigh, and on the way, like a swimmer, come up for air along the hip or belly. Continue along the contour a little, then submerge again and fade out inside the thigh. Do the same up through the torso into each arm, breaking surface as you move into and through the shoulder. Work in this way moving from drawing to drawing, until the figures are filled out. Change colour after each round.

Drift contours

Do you remember the peripheral exercises, and keeping your eyes constantly on what you are seeing?

Now, choosing a coloured chalk that is sharp enough, begin to follow the contours downward, using long drift-lines. Choose a beginning, then draw with your eyes on the contour continuously, drawing as if touching, in one long stroke. As you draw, see whether you can tune into the drift. Don't 'think' it – just allow eye and hand to be open to the possibility of entering it, sliding down along this natural trace on the threshold of possibility, the north face of perception. Continue, changing colours for each round, until the contours, short ones as well, are complete. You don't draw around the head, but rather choose and follow the drift of one strand of hair, then another. If you see the profile, go into reverse and try drawing upward in this same way. Complete the contours only as far as the inner form is completed.

Place the drawings in close sequence on the wall.

These figures stand erect, and are full of fire and energy. Though they are footless, they stand well – more securely upright than many a 'finished' drawing of a standing figure feet and all. They witness that the source of the pose determines how well a figure stands, and that source in the centre.

Colour is a new, added dimension. Why does colour give this enormous pleasure? What is colour, after all? It is time to find out.

The Children of Light

'I want to know one thing.
What is colour?

Pablo Picasso

X enobiologists (people who think about life on other planets) argue that on any world with life and light, sight will evolve to see it. Sight, like flight, is a 'universal', says Dr Jack Cohen. He thinks so because sight here on earth evolved on so many separate paths. Chordates (all us vertebrates), insects and crustaceans can all see – molluscs alone have at least six kinds of eyes, each with a separate origin. Vision happened, over and over, via their autonomous evolutionary histories. The eye of the octopus is similar to the human eye in many respects, yet it evolved with no connection to us, independently.

Light and sight

Colour needs an observer, and colour in living things paralleled the development of colour vision among nature's creatures. The purpose of the flower is to perpetuate itself. Its colours are evolved with bees in mind and their eyes are very different from ours. That we enjoy the colours of flowers, and even how we see them, is unimportant to the flower. Here is a poem about that, which I wrote after watching a TV series called *How Animals See*:

This is terrible.
It says here
bees can't see yellow.
So the broom, the rape, even the dusty
stamen of the rose
are lurid puce, a shuddery ultra pink,
studied to perfection
over hot millennia how best
to please their lust,
these bits
zooming in for the take
faceted fuzzy cells
the dancing optic of a vast
seduced intelligence.
And as for us
what the flower intends
Is less than casual –
utter indifference.
Oh my notched, loved world, atlas of lies,
no longer fit to believe!
and not even mine, not private –
photographed, reassured –
Van Gogh in Arles –
impassioned cadmiums!
Armfuls of buttercups
plundered in childhood

on the Musqueam flats!
And now this maple, frost of gold!!
The bees are gone to hive,
in secret, they keep the real real,
their tiny manifold eye
closing in on
the actual valuable
planet, terrible in neon and violet.

The evolution of sight

Vision evolved in the distant past. It must have started with organisms learning to detect the difference between light and dark. This function is still the basis of vision.

Picture the far distant past – broad daylight, a moving shadow, the reappearance of light.

Sight was definitely a good strategy for survival. A simple photoreceptor – hardly more than a patch of pigment on the forepart of some rudimentary brain – reacted to a passing shadow, and transmitted on and off signals to two bipolar cells, one for darkness and one for light. With one kind of cone or photoreceptor, an organism could determine this much; add more kinds and more complexity and different signals could be compared. For some of God's creatures, on a variety of evolutionary paths, colour arrived – on the scene and in the brain.

Colour is recent history

How important is colour? We can recognize objects without its aid in line drawings and monochromatic photos, which indicates that shape and boundaries are the prime informants. As with a black-and-white TV, most of the brain's energy is spent on the patterning, and it does not take much more power to add colour to this basic circuitry. Colour, in terms of neural effort, comes in as an extra, a 'frill'. The experience of *colour shock* has not been studied under fMRIs as far as I know, but surely it would show sudden activity, wild excitement in a previously dormant V4 (the colour centre), almost overloading the circuits.

The premise that colour is an addition or enhancement is in some ways borne out in our careers as artists. For many, drawing is still regarded as the basic skill, the foundation, like playing scales and arpeggios for the musician – a preliminary to the 'real thing' of the concert. For many artists, *colour shock* means that precise, explosive moment after years of working mostly in tone, when the glory of colour hits them like a revelation. They can point to the exact time in their lives this occurred. For Paul Klee it was in 1914 in Tunisia: 'Colour has taken possession of me; no longer do I have to chase after it, I know that it has hold of me forever,' was his famous statement. 'Colour and I are one. I am a painter.'

Yet the colourless, bounding line continues to entrance us, and monochrome, tended with devotion or returned to like an old love, has wonderful depths and qualities of its own. Most of the universe, after all, is colourless. We live in the precincts of the rainbow, in a narrow band of sunlight that scatters in the air, transilluminates water, and reflects off the surfaces of the world. Below the human scale and beyond it forever, in the atomic realm and in the astronomical deeps of space, there is no colour, only light and darkness. In the story of creation, God did not declare 'Let there be colour,' but 'Let there be light.' In fact, in the Bible, or any other ancient texts, colours are not mentioned at all. Colour – even the concept of colour – is very recent in human history. Until about 500 AD, colours were not even part of the vocabulary. People simply did not think in terms of colour – although they were not colour-blind, as Gladstone thought, when nineteenth-century scholars such as Mueller noted the surprising absence of colour-terms in old texts.

Brightness not hue

It's hard for us now to realize that distinguishing colour by its brightness has been almost the universal norm. Aristotle was the first to distinguish colours, and described two – blue, which he said appeared out of darkness, and yellow, which appeared out of light. Now, we discriminate colour by hue, but the Aristotelian scale was in degrees of luminance. Each colour was thought to be formed by the admixture of dark (black) or light (white).

The ordering of colour

In Medieval Europe four colours were identified, based on the four elements. Arbitrary colour-sets multiplied. The only thing they had in common seemed to be that they were derived from the urge to make a colour-set. By the sixth century the mystical number seven was being applied across the board to classify animals, humours, temperaments, planets and colours too. In 1637 Newton, with his prism, divided sunlight by its wavelengths into seven. Kepler, obsessed with the idea of universal harmony, likened the seven-hued spectrum to the musical scale. Later, theorists could not get the seventh colour (indigo) to 'fit', and proposed six. Most European languages name eleven or twelve. English has eleven. There are about three thousand words in usage for various shades of colour, and people are said to be able to distinguish thousands, some say up to a million, different hues.

Colour systems and colour meanings abound today. The choice of warm or cool colours is said to separate the extrovert from the introvert. Students of the chakra assign colours to different areas of the body, and healers apply them to different diseases. Colour steeps the history of religious ceremony and pageantry. The psychology of colour – how colour affects mood – is a flourishing industry, spilling over from health sciences to interior decoration, fashion, manufacture and architecture.

If you have studied colour theory in the field of art, you've probably been puzzled already by its subjectivity – its varieties of wheels, maps, chips, charts, primaries, secondaries, saturations, brightnesses and hues. It helps to remember that through most of history people got by without noticing colours at all.

Before colour

In ancient Greece colour was not considered on its own, but was always context specific – an integral part of the object seen or described. This meant that words we define as free-floating colours were once the names of objects. Purple (*purfurios*) was a dye or cloth, writes Eleanor Irwin in *Colour Terms in Greek Poetry*. The 'wearing of the purple' is a phrase you'd still understand as referring to the stuff rather than the colour. Scarlet was also a cloth once, and you could perfectly well have brown scarlets and green scarlets. The word *roan* is still specific for a certain-coloured horse.

Words which later came to mean colours stood for other

attributes of the surfaces of the visible world. *Purfurios* was not the red-blue hue we think of as purple, but instead a kind of slow shimmering or undulation, like the sheen on wafted silk or the breaking light from the bow wave of a ship. Before the more limited idea of green (*chloros*) as a hue, the word meant anything fresh and flexible and could describe a girl's neck, or newly spilled blood.

These attributes or components were significant to the people who used them, in the ordering or categorizing of their world. What was important to them was the quality of surfaces – their lustre, gloss, or iridescence, and the extremes of brightness and darkness. Mediterranean sunlight is intense and it's understandable to describe a tree as 'dark-leaved' rather than 'green-leaved'. Greeks ordered their universe in polarities – up or down, light or dark, male or female. We use polarity now when we classify colours as cool or warm.

Even the rainbow, in myths and folklore, was not celebrated for its many colours. For Homer it has one colour, purple, which as we have seen was not a hue at all but a kind of iridescence. The rainbow's shape was what was important – as bridge or bow, connecting gods and mortals, the sign of reconciliation. It was promise and prophecy, the subject of legends and a forecaster of weather. To point at a rainbow was unlucky and could cause your finger to wither. Its colours were unimportant or ignored. An old Finnish rhyme admits two:

> *A pure sail is on a cloud,*
> *A red goose is on the sail,*
> *The goose has a blue tail.*

The bands of the rainbow

Nowadays, when you look at the rainbow, you can see bands of definable colour. Yet there are no bands.

The rainbow is a continuous spectrum, a merging of varying wavelength. How do you categorize a domain with no boundaries? Such a domain needs salient landmarks. We learn to make the divisions, and so to see them, to some extent through the structure of our visual system, and to some extent through our culture. There is disagreement as to how much the structure contributes, but the mechanism of sight seems to have a bearing on colour vocabulary – on where, on the rainbow, the name applies and where the boundary is placed. Physically, we do have three types of cones extracting information about the three 'primary' colours, so seeing each one and naming it right in the 'middle' (where it appears most salient) would be logical.

There is a fair consensus among languages as far as this goes. Yet languages vary enormously both to the number of 'bands' distinguished and to where the boundaries between the bands are placed. The Russians have two words for blue. The Musqueam of British Columbia have one word for yellow and green. It's been put forward that low-technology groups don't distinguish between green and blue. High-tech cultures, on the other hand, need to focus in the cone-rich centre of the eye, and thus develop an increasingly elaborate system of colour names. This 'evolutionary' concept of colour has been called narrowly Eurocentric, and there are many examples to disprove it.

Words for colour in different languages have a hierarchy, as recorded by Berlin and Kay in their exhaustive study which started off all the arguments over thirty years ago. First come white and black (or light and dark) and to some groups, like the pre-Aristotelian Greeks, these are sufficient. If there is one more colour named, it will always be red. If one more, it will be yellow or green, and the next will be blue. Colours can be differentiated almost ad infinitum. We can bring in modifiers, adjectives to further describe brightness and chromatic purity. In tests, it's found that people choose emotional modifiers over ones about straight luminance or saturation, and shy away from using more than one at once, which perhaps is an admonition to poets.

What is your favourite colour? Try applying these or other adjectives to it. How does the addition of a modifier change its appearance and its affect (or feel), in your mind's eye?

Pallid, dusky, washed out, hazy, murky, gloomy, subdued.

Vivid, intense, vibrant, glowing, dense, flamboyant, fierce.

Choose your colour and one adjective from the above. Write it down on paper and use chalks or watercolour to depict it.

Names, as we have learned, are of prime importance in our efforts to order, categorize and remember – they label the invariants. No one is born with the ability to see arbitrary bands in a continuous rainbow spectrum. No wonder children have a hard time recognizing 'colours'. The ability to get colours straight (for their culture) is normally achieved by the age of four, and naming is the glue which helps children remember them. The language of the culture we are born into 'creates' the different colours we see.

What then is colour?

We all know the answer to that. Or do we? It might be an idea to define it, just as we defined line.

> *Think of a definition for colour. Don't take too long, as colour, the concept of colour, is very complex indeed. There is no one definition. Try answering the following questions:*
>
> *How do different colours make you feel?*
> *Where is this colour found?*

An important aspect of colour is its emotional effect. The sheer enjoyment of colour is surely central to any definition of it. When you answered 'Where is colour found?' you probably mentioned objects or their surfaces, because we structure the world according to objects, and their shape–colour bond identifies them for us. A more sophisticated answer would be in terms of light – we can't see colours unless there is light to see them by, and colour is composed of the various wavelengths of light. Or something about the eyes and the brain – because without perception, colours do not 'really' exist at all.

Colour constancy

Remember when you looked at your two hands and learned how the brain performed a trick to make their size appear constant, despite your moving them? Appearances can differ from reality if reality is a problem. Obviously, dexterity is important; it's much easier to handle things when our hands stay the same size, so the brain compensates. When it comes to compensation the brain has more tricks up its sleeve, like *colour constancy*.

Picture a red apple hanging on a tree in all weathers, then plucked and placed indoors on a green, blue or white plate.

Ambient (surrounding) light undergoes extreme changes, and in changing light the apple's surface reflects not just one, stable wavelength – it is all over the map. Yet we do experience it as a stable, particular red. This is because our visual system, having to function under a range of light conditions, and needing to recognize objects against many different backgrounds, has found out how to override these differences. This ability is called *discounting the illuminant* and its result is *colour constancy* – the perception of colours as stable, despite their changing physical properties in ambient light. The visual system compares and compensates, weighs and measures, takes everything into account (including the wavelength of the light surrounding the apple), and through a complex process comes up with the consistent red we recognize, whatever the light.

Different pathways from the retina handle different kinds of information at different levels. In the retina itself, the ratio-taking operation is *achromatic* – indifferent to colour. Colour information is passed on but not interfered with en route – it is left to make its way through to the higher cortex, the colour centre V4. Only there in V4 is colour finally perceived.

Constancy and art
The painter must struggle with how human vision interprets the visual world. Imagine the difficulty of reproducing, in a

laboratory, any equivalent of the transient, visual world, with all the vagaries and variations of the outdoors and its changing light!

Imagine looking across a meadow at a wood on a bright day, just as a cloud passes over. Imagine intending to make a painting.

The part of the wood in shadow is far different from the part drenched in sunlight. What happens in a small, localized area may be scattered, blown apart and obliterated by the global impact of the whole. The mechanisms of colour constancy are on overload in their attempt to reduce and accommodate. You have only your vision to help you and it will change everything if it can. Where do you go from here?

Colour is not a science

In the philosophy of colour, there is no one answer. Colour cannot be a precise science, or even a science at all, because it can never be physically pinned down, like, for example, weight or liquidity. It depends on the observer and every observer with eyesight is an expert – is in fact, the only expert – because without what colour looks like to you, and me, and everyone, it would not exist and would have no interest whatsoever.

Colour is seen, and we can study what causes colour to be seen. It's possible to explain physical cause and effect – for example, why there are no bluish-yellows, or reddish-greens. But colour cannot be adequately defined by its structure alone. There are no colour thermometers, only people who experience it. And because colour is not an objective feature of the world, we can't make a science of colour itself. We can only wander around the outskirts and look at it from various angles and poke at it.

The natural concept of colour

The *natural concept of colour* encourages you to take what's called an 'objective' view. There are some 'plain truths' everyone surely agrees on. Colour is a physical property of the world which our eyes are sensitive to. At the naïve level, objects 'have' colour.

We certainly *experience* colour as a property of objects. Colours have names and we can learn them. Given the structure of human vision, and our ability to test it, and given cultural consensus, we are able to communicate our experience of colour. It can be organized into identifiable parts which relate to each other in specific ways. And we relate to colour – socially, aesthetically and emotionally. According to this theory, we have *prime intuitions* about it. We know that it is not hidden but *manifest*. It's there.

The *illusion concept of colour*

According to the *illusion concept of colour*, this is not so. Colour has no features in nature at all. It is simply not out there. It has no properties which are independent of the perceiver. It does not exist. To see colour is a 'false consciousness'. However, it can be said to have 'virtual properties' and can operate through these perfectly well, and so it does not need real ones. It's quite sufficient that things appear to be coloured; they need not really be so. The colour red is not red, but has the power to *appear* red to the right perceiver. In this way we live 'as if it were so'.

It is as if...

For the bees it's something else, and with no bees something else again, or nothing at all. Colour, in the long evolutionary view, is that property of the environment which makes colour happen in an animal's vision. It relates to the kind of eyes that see it and therefore we humans with our human eyes can't grasp that it's relative. Nor can the bees.

You experience colour as out there in three-dimensional space. It seems so, just as when you hurt your foot you feel that pain down there in your foot. We project colour and we project pain, neither of which really exist as physical entities, and this is very smart of us after all.

It's exasperating and fun to think about colour. These theories – which have many sets and subsets – generate great arguments among their followers. You the viewer, in this case you the artist, are free to choose all or any according to your temperament. It's nice to know that your own vision is the expert and arbiter, and that whatever you learn about colour you end up right back here, wide-eyed on your own threshold.

Senses that overlap

Synaesthesia, a condition in which a stimulation of one sense triggers a response in another, is common in children and in about one in two thousand adults. To give an example, for me hearing the tone F elicits the visual sensation of a warm, rather thick yellow like pea soup. Words, numbers, and individual letters can 'have' colours. A synaesthete does not consider these perceptions extraordinary and may not even be particularly aware of them. They are said to be involuntary, and can persist from childhood throughout life. Synaesthetes tend to be creative, and their colourful images assist their memory. If shown a letter in the 'right' colour (the one they associate it with) they will read it at lightning speed. If shown the letter differently coloured, their response is slowed down by inhibitory cells which light up in a cortical area known as the *anterior cingulate*. The 'right' colour is experienced in the mind, and does not interfere with seeing the viewed letter. But the synaesthete knows when a letter has the 'wrong' colour and finds it difficult to read. Whether some cells devoted to the other sense actually are found in both visual areas, or whether they are able to activate across boundaries, is not clear.

Choose a bright red crayon or felt pen. Take some cards or small pieces of paper. Write the word RED on one, using the crayon liberally. On another, write the word GREEN, and on another, BLUE. Now choose a green crayon and do the same again with more cards or paper. Repeat the whole thing using blue.

Be aware – ask yourself: was writing the word in the 'right' colour easier than writing it in a different colour?

Mix the nine cards up and look at them in turn. Name aloud the colour the words are written in. See how quick (or how slow) you are at saying the name of each colour. Go through them again, this time reading aloud each written word. Be aware again of any differences in time and effort.

Artists in all fields use cross-sensual imagery when they talk about their art. Goethe was a famous synaesthete who wrote that colour and sound were 'like two rivers which have their source on one and the same mountain'. Rimbaud, Litzt, Nabokov, David Hockney and many others have described their synaesthesia and its relation to their creativity. Kandinsky was a close friend of Shostakovich and they corresponded about the relationships between music and colour. In his passionate dissertations on colours, Kandinsky called them sounds 'causing vibrations in the soul'. Intervals and associations, chords and harmonies were the property of both arts, and each art illuminated the other. Yellow for Kandinsky was 'a high-pitched fanfare' and black 'eternal silence'.

Oliver Sacks writes that the brain is highly flexible, and signals can be exchanged between the separate areas controlling visual and aural impressions. Studies of the congenitally deaf show how the brain will pre-empt unexpected regions for new functions. In the deaf, the left temporal lobe (used for auditory processing in hearing people) is reassigned for vision and becomes active in signing. Many blind people use hearing to visualize the world: for example, a friend of mine sings aloud when entering a strange house, walking from room to room and 'seeing' each one's acoustic shape. Something like this may be happening involuntarily in the overlapping and intermingling of the senses in the brains of synaesthetes.

Whether you are a full-blown synaesthete or not, you can respond creatively to the association of colour and sound, just as you respond to colour in terms of feeling. Baudelaire wrote that he would have been far more surprised if it were otherwise – if 'sound could *not* suggest colour, that colours could not evoke the idea of a melody, and that sound and colour were unsuitable for the translation of ideas, seeing that things have always found their expression through a system of reciprocal analogy.'

> *Look out across the room. Make a conscious decision to 'listen' to white. Do the same for black. Then red. Listen to other colours, your attention quietly ready to allow them priority one by one.*
>
> *Take a walk through a market, or a garden, or past brightly lit stores. Choose one colour and listen to it attentively.*
>
> *As you walk, listen to the sound of voices. Of traffic. What else do you hear? What colour does it call to mind? Can you pay attention to a sound and a colour simultaneously? Which colour would seep in and stain which sound most effectively?*

The artist's attention can be directed by choice. Playing with your attention will stretch and enliven it. Anything out there, attended to, responds a thousandfold, in storms of generosity.

The binding problem

In our daily experience, colour is inextricably bound to shape. A lemon is yellow. Whatever else is going on in our visual system (and a great deal else is) things-and-the-colour-of-things coexist as we live our lives, seeing them in the world or imagining them. The colour of an object 'fills it in' to its edges, and then stops. This is our understanding of how it is, and works for us well enough.

What is happening (or not happening) in the visual brain? The colour centre V4 is quite separate from the orientation centre, which consists of cells indifferent to colour and devoted to translating edges into lines. This riddle of how they exist for us as one, called the binding problem, exercises neurologists greatly at present and is as yet unresolved.

It is argued there must be as-yet-undiscovered cells in the higher visual cortex sensitive to both colour and shape, simply because this is how things *are*. Natural images have colour and shape, and natural images must have had a say in how sight evolved to see them. Even a boundary is defined by both colour and tone, and therefore you have to assume that somewhere in the brain there are neurons which get excited by both. We just haven't found them yet.

These are the questions: how can two different but parallel systems – in a sense, two separate consciousnesses – come to be experienced as inextricably united? And what happens when artists provocatively tear them apart?

Colour-and-shape in art

Our daily experience carries quite naturally through into pictures and picture-making at any level – witness the popularity of colouring books for children (who try to get so good at it they don't 'go over the edges') or the easier computer counterpart, where they can choose a colour and click on the appropriate shape, and it instantly fills itself in. Then there is 'paint by numbers' for aspiring hobby painters, exploiting the same requirement and using the same method.

Until recently in the history of painting, this coherence was taken for granted. As pigments became stabilized this 'picture-book' clarity (object plus its undiluted colour) was the rule. Later, chiaroscuro (and coats of heavy varnish) moved painting more towards tone. The Impressionists were the first to employ colour 'scientifically', though they still attached it to objects – their idea was to re-create patches of pure colour uncontaminated by their surrounding colours, painting every point in isolation, its wavelength recorded faithfully or even exaggerated. (Though among the Impressionists and Post-Impressionists no one abided strictly to rule, and Cézanne was somewhere else entirely.) With Expressionism and Fauvism, painters stopped being concerned about copying colours from nature; Expressionists used colours for emotional impact, and the Fauvists deliberately chose the 'wrong' colour for objects. Since then, with the advent of abstract and non-objective painting, colour has been freed from its dependence on recognizable shape.

Impressionism

Are you familiar with this experience? As you walk through one of the great galleries, going from the Romantics to the Impressionists can be like passing from a gloomy hallway into sunlight. What is this difference? Somehow, light has come back into the picture, back into colour.

The Impressionists and Neo-Impressionists studied and experimented with new theories about the optics of colour. Cerveul, a French chemist working on dyes, systematized colours by wavelength, and was the one of the first to try to explain the active role of the brain in colour perception. His *Law of Simultaneous Contrast* states that two colours, placed adjacently, will always appear as dissimilar as possible. This means that if you wanted to change a colour, just change the colour of its background. His system took into account variations in intensity and saturation as well – how the same colour will appear brighter on a darker ground, and darker against a lighter one, and how a greyed colour will appear stronger (more saturated) against grey, and weaker against colour. The Impressionists reasoned that if perception can perform these contrasts, the palette can perform them too. Colour could now be approached by painters as a kind of science – the science of how wavelength light, unaltered, behaves or is perceived according to its setting.

Pointillism as a practice dependent on this rule – that light received from adjacent patches of colours will mix in the retina to form a more luminous colour than if the primary colours were first mixed on the palette. Even the size of the patches (or dots) of colour was controlled to depend on a fixed viewing distance – about three times the picture's diagonal – where they would appear to fuse. Just before or at that threshold, in the effort of the eye to focus, the colours would seem to vibrate and tremble in rivalry, and the painting would achieve its maximum lustre and luminosity.

In ordinary perception, the brain's work of constancy discounts the illuminant and we see stable colours. The Impressionists deliberately counted ambient light back in. Patches of pure wavelength colour, each uncontaminated by its surround and placed as if in isolation are, after all, what the retina receives. The retina of the observer, gazing at the canvas, receives them as if it was receiving the natural scene. The global effect of an entire canvas painted in this way is dazzling.

Encounters

If you paint, you know about the behaviour of complementary colours and have experimented with them. The first conscious encounter with pure wavelength colour is unforgettable. For me it occurred while I was making a self-portrait in rather bad light. I was staring into the mirror at an area near the left eye. It looked (it *was* – I perceived it so) shadowy, dull and colourless. As I stared, I remember making a tiny act of decision, or attention – a kind of step into space. As if I had passed through into the unknown, and then left myself there and got out of the way. What colour was I looking at? Not influenced, or expected, or predicted, or intended, not even longed for. What was it? It was deep, bright red. (It *was* – I perceived it so.)

The great Impressionists and Neo-Impressionists brought to their work not just theories of optics, but also themselves, their creativity. Monet deliberately exaggerated the wavelength colours to express changes in light. Renoir said, 'I want my red to sound like a bell. If I do not achieve it, I put in more red, and other colours, until I've got it.' Whatever Seurat or Signac intended, they were not mindless factories churning out replicas of the visual wavelengths of the world. Their work shows how personal genius persists in spite of everything – in their case, in spite of how they required themselves to represent the effects of natural light, as accurately as they could, by using unmixed little points or dots of pure paint on canvas. Cézanne was the master; in his work every colour resonates with every other colour in a new existence, in what Rilke called a 'beyond of colour, without previous memories'.

The lesson needs repeating. If you search for truth it will be your truth. Truth in terms of your visual system and the passion and commitment you have for attaining it. You do not need to concern yourself with the personal. The personal will take good care of itself.

Beyond Expressionism

With the onset of non-objective painting, colour became the property of artists in a new way. In imitation of the brain, as a kind of externalization of it, colour can manage – and thrive – on its own, unbound by the recognizable object or any object, unconstricted by line. Yves Klein said that line is only 'colour compressed', that colour is line 'expanded and exploded.' He saw this emancipation of colour as a kind of return to Eden. The Expulsion meant being 'mastered by the invasion of line, imprisoned, compartmentalized, cut apart'. He called pure colour 'the universal soul in which the human soul is bathing in a state of earthly paradise'.

The riddle

The image of nearing the early stages of the visual process is a powerful one. Intercepting and recording wavelength colour before the constancy mechanisms get hold of it meant, for the Impressionists, getting closer to the source – the light hitting the eye. Is this possible? According to the structure of the visual system it is not – conscious perception of colour does not happen at the retina but further in, when the constancy mechanisms have done their work and not before. This is the riddle. You could say that Cerveul's meticulous investigation and systemization of colour provided artists with both information about how the system works, and a means to replicate it. According this argument, what is there on the canvas isn't what they saw, but a systematized breakdown of *what they were told they saw before they saw it* – which happens to be correct. And this makes these 'spontaneous, retinal' painters jotting down their 'impressions' of the natural world the most cerebral painters of all. We know that Monet spent many, many thoughtful hours indoors working on his differently lighted views of the Opera and the cathedral at Rouen. In *Inner Vision*, neurologist Semir Zeki has written a fascinating investigation of Monet's brain and concludes that Monet painted 'with his intelligence'. The riddle however persists – painters, with attention, can see contextual colour out of context. When I chose to, I did *see* that red. My experience is all I have.

Tone

Our perception of brightness is also relative. Just as the brain stabilizes colour, it stabilizes tone. Though these two attributes of vision are processed separately, and end up in different areas of the cortex, they have parallel pathways. The actual wavelength lightness and brightness (reflectance and luminance) hitting our eyes undergoes similar alterations to end up with stability. For example, the TV screen in neutral is a sort of fuzzy medium grey. When we switch to a programme it brightens – and at the same time, even though the darkest images on the screen remain that same grey, we perceive them as black.

With luminance, there is an interesting hitch. It's called *simultaneous lightness contrast* or SLC – and it's a constancy mechanism gone somewhat haywire. SLC means that the same grey appears darker against a lighter ground and lighter against a darker one. I mean, darker and lighter than it reasonably 'should' and different by comparison.

You can test this by cutting out two patches of medium-grey paper, and laying one (be sure it's completely flat) on a lighter grey card, and one on a darker grey. Compare them. You won't believe your eyes. Exchange the two patches to be sure. Try mixing patches with paint and applying similar ones to lighter or darker backgrounds. It's almost impossible to get it 'right', given that, depending on the background, 'right' is definitely 'wrong'.

Tonal values in art

Problems with drawing light and shade on the model, or managing tonal values in painting, must arise in part from this dance of SLC – how the perception of a tone, which 'ought' to be stabilized in our perception, may be out of synch. You might imagine a large drawing of a model lit by a strong spotlight, with a lot of shadow. Looking deep into the shadow discounts the illuminant, and tonal variations and details appear. SLC overcompensates in your perception of them and you are unable to balance lights and darks. I have seen something like this happen in drawings of the shadowed underside of the nose. In order to accommodate dark nostrils the nose is left light, like the lighter grey card. And I have heard loud claims that the nostrils are black and the surround much lighter, which compel me to accept that they must be perceived so. Yet when looked at globally, looked at in contrast with even the rest of the face, the whole shadowed area 'appears' evenly grey.

Handling tone is also an important skill for painters. Seurat, for all he was a sublime colourist, was also deeply engaged in the effect of tone, and a master at the interplay of values. It's been said that the test of a painting is how satisfying it is reproduced in black and white. This is probably why Monet's famous lily-ponds leave me cold, especially compared to his late, hot, deeply toned paintings.

At the skin of the eye

We are the children of light. Now we have speculated about coming closer to the uncontaminated, not yet interfered with, earliest stages of vision and how, if we could do so, or even imagine we were doing so, we'd have a better chance at seeing that light – what is 'really' there. This may just be an image – picturing the way the eye is out in front of the brain and the skin of the eye is actually touching the outside world. Can we get closer to that threshold? Giacometti was the ultimate literal artist; his quest was to get at the truth of what he saw – 'More true,' he said, 'ever always more true.' His quest was unending and despairing. 'You would have to die of it.'

How close did he come? Could one get so close that even the unconscious beginnings of colour perception were preceded? Is this possible?

Malevich famously spoke of the sky as *liberated* from its blue to become white – 'broken through and entered white, the true, real conception of infinity'. Giacometti said, 'If I see everything in grey, and in grey all the colours which I experience and which I would like to express, then why should I use any other colour? It was never my intention to paint only with grey. But in the course of my work I have eliminated one colour after another, and what has remained is grey.'

Can it be that in striving for the truth of that unknown, external world, one is forced to discard even colour like a broken toy?

The Embodied Mind

'The brain keeps its repertoire, even what is not very useful. There is a difference between junk and garbage.'

Semir Zeki

U p to now we have been exploring perception, the act of sight, and it might seem as though the imagination has come in for a lot of flak. You have been told that the brain top-downs generalized information which interferes rather than assists. That there is a quarrel, a struggle at least, between what is coming in and what is so tenaciously there.

The brain's way of seeing is all we have. Yet the act of sight, the work of sight, seems to involve this continuous argument between the unknown and the recognized. Until now we have been exploring ways of paying attention to the unknown – asking questions such as: what is out there? how can I see it? how do I see it? how do I resist my brain's determination to pre-empt and restructure – should I even try? and is not my quest in creating art the same as my brain's – to make something *permanent* and *understandable* and satisfying?

These words, even the word *beautiful*, aren't strong

enough to describe what I want to create. *Permanent* enough to be looked at by myself and others. *Understandable*, in whatever medium, in terms of itself – its visible structure, composition, colour, texture, form – a contained whole. *Satisfying*, just the way the brain finds the invariant representation satisfying.

'Bad' art

Unsatisfactory or 'bad' art is never glaringly or interestingly bad. On the contrary, it lacks interest, or any kind of *glare* at all, positive or negative. It is mediocre.

'Bad' art is dishonest. It is lost somewhere between the visible world and the invariant, and those who make it are muddling them up and not paying much attention to either. Visual psychologists call it the *Perky effect* – the interference of mental imagery with perception, which results in a real, measurable reduction of visual sensitivity. In experiments, the Perky effect enables subjects to read without even noticing words with jumbled letters – and except for proofreaders this nimble ability has its uses. Mostly you can trust the brain's predictions, so its capacity to fill-in and take short-cuts makes good sense.

But what about art? Here the Perky effect results in inaccuracies so common and so predictable that they make for boring (not satisfying or interesting, hence 'bad') drawing. You already have the example of the line 'hopping' from object to object in the predictable places. Misjudging size, raising the head, isolating named areas – these are all instances of the Perky effect, where the brain's image has blurred the sight. Another one is making lines around sexually significant areas or colouring them darkly in.

Much time is spent criticizing and correcting these supposed 'errors'. And if the results of the Perky effect show up and cause trouble here, we can expect them anywhere in our art. Their persistence suggests purpose. Maybe in some sense they are not 'wrong' after all. At any rate, it's interesting and instructive to take a closer look and try to understand what is happening.

Tiny hands and feet

In the case of hands and feet, the usual complaint is that they are drawn 'too small'. Is there a not-in-scale image in the brain, and if so why? Is it because, as babies, we experienced these distal parts as far-away entities, out there at the ends of our limbs? They are the extensions into, and manipulators of, a distant, outside world. *Hand* equals *small object*. With our feet there is the additional problem of always seeing from one angle, from above, which makes us conceive of them as flat.

Take a moment to experience your hands. Close your eyes. Sense them at the ends of your arms and form a mental image of them. Still with closed eyes, press finger and thumb together and again sense and 'see' the apposition.

This *feel* of your hands with its internal image of them will seem correct to you. It isn't, but *keep it in mind* – as of course you do anyway.

The needle of passion

Hands are important, maybe even more important than we

realize. There is a cartoon diagram of the corticular surface, showing how much of it is devoted to each sense. It's called the *sensory homunculus*. The area for touch is enormous. Hands and feet are hugely represented. The simple apposition – forefinger and thumb – takes up more than a sixth of the whole surface.

But our mental image of the apposition is of convergence, extreme compression into a tiny, working point – the fine-tuning of tools and touching and delineation. That our feet seem to share this image with the hands is the legacy of ancestors who clung to trees and grasped with their toes as well as their fingers. We know – from the proficiency attained by people denied the use of fingers – that toes have the same latent ability. In the mental image of the body, hands and (potentially) feet are narrowing, convergent points for the compression of enormous energies that are forced to follow the command of our attention, as if through a chasm or even a needle's eye.

'The eye of the needle of passion is narrow,' said Rumi. And Giacometti said, 'I have to make a little hole in nature.'

Looking at our hands

Seeing our hands, the day-to-day experience of them, ought to set things right, but strangely enough this is no help. Something called *perceptual constancy* conspires to distort our vision. Remember how, in exploring depth and space, you held up your two hands? Do so again.

Hold your hands up in front of you, one about a foot from your eyes, and one further away. Move them about.

The space you can reach into with your hands (it's the space represented in still-life paintings) is called *domestic* or *kinetic* space. Within it, the brain alters our perception so we can more easily *handle* things. We are so used to this compensatory trick we don't notice it. But consider what it entails. The brain, for these two particular objects, changes its circuitry in a drastic way. Actually, a hand held close to the eyes occludes (covers and blots out) much more of the rest of the field than one held farther off. The retina is receiving the correct information; yet we see something else entirely – two hands the same size.

A reality check

This distortion applies only to your own hands, possibly with tools held so habitually they've become somatic extensions.

> *Try some other pairs of objects – for example books, or apples, placed at various distances from your eyes in the domestic space. What about someone else's hands? What about your hands if someone else, standing behind you, moves them for you? What about, if you are agile enough, your feet?*
>
> *To convince yourself of the height of the foot, try grasping it over the arch.*
>
> *Now try this arm-hand measurement. Divide by three, from underarm to elbow, elbow to wrist, wrist to fingertips.*

It might come as a shock to find that the foot has so much height, and that the hand-wrist length is one third. A hand is a surprisingly large object – its span covers the face. The foot is not flat, and it too is large – the length of a head. Yet in confronting our fixed ideas, even reality checks like this don't seem to help.

Change by exaggeration

It's beginning to look as if drawing hands and feet the right size is more complicated than you thought. And resisting the disproportion and trying to change it seems self-defeating. Fritz Perls claimed that resistance just doesn't work. To change inappropriate behaviour it's better to exaggerate it, enjoy it and play it for all it's worth. 'You can never overcome anything by resisting it. Whatever it is, if you go deeply enough into it, it will disappear; it will be assimilated. If you are spiteful, be more spiteful. If you are performing, increase the performance.'

Perhaps this advice can be applied to drawing. Take the example of the hands and feet. What if, instead of resisting, instead of trying (against all inclination) to draw them bigger, you decided to draw them small on purpose – extremely, ridiculously, impossibly small? Could exaggerating the 'fault' have some effect on it and make it go away?

Use a mirror or the model, and be sure you can see at least three distal parts (hands, feet). Draw the whole figure. Draw as well as you can, making a solid, unified form. Draw hands and feet last, and very carefully. Have fun with all the details – even the nails. But make them very small in comparison to the rest of the figure.

Surprises

With a drawing made purposely out of scale, you'd expect the results to be negative – this is a drawing to labour through, laugh at, learn from, and discard. You made it as an experiment, perhaps considering the whole idea a waste of time. Yet two surprising things happened: first, if you genuinely and attentively completed this figure with its very small hands and feet, you ended up with a drawing of interest, even of beauty; and second, it was fun.

Why is such a drawing beautiful? And if it is all wrong, how can it be fun to make?

Perhaps you were cautious and did not make the hands or feet that much smaller than usual. Perhaps you didn't allow yourself to take it seriously, or to draw attentively, or to enjoy getting into the tiny parts. If you're 'good at drawing' you felt impatient, because you already know the proportions and don't make mistakes.

Make one more drawing. This time, write VERY SMALL HANDS/FEET on the paper to help you stick with it. When you get to the hands and feet, let yourself enjoy drawing them, and be aware of what sensations arise.

Somatic excitement

Getting into the minuscule forms, working with extreme delicacy and accuracy, is oddly delightful. When I first made such a drawing, I expected to hate doing it. But as I got into the nitty-gritty details I could feel a curious somatic excitement, a simmering – my own fingers and toes even began to tingle.

Where does this excitement come from? The invariant representation, obviously. The image cascades down the visual pathway, for once unresisted, for once allowed – even invited – to take over. What makes these drawings beautiful is your whole-hearted, conscious acceptance of the invariant. The invariant representation has its own truth because it is there, as it is, in your brain.

It seems that to draw 'wrong' is not simply to be lazy or stupid and obstinate. Rather it's to be loyal to a truth that is different from, and can be stronger than, the truth of the incoming visual information. If you draw hands and feet too small as a rule, it's because your brain is telling you to. You might check out what you see from time to time, but you are not going to accept the actual scale.

Commitment and responsibility

These last drawings are interesting and beautiful, however, in a way that ordinary drawings with their predictable 'error' of underscaled hands and feet are definitely not. Why?

If you compare 'ordinary' disproportionate drawings with these new ones, you will find an important difference. When you consciously commit yourself to the invariant, *choose* it, and take responsibility for that choice – you are into opening up all sorts of creative possibilities. Working attentively across the perceptual boundaries, you can produce nervy, exciting visual images that the observer understands as true – *true* to the consensual imagination of the human body.

So, when you chose not to resist the 'error' but to go deeper into it, it did in one sense 'disappear': it ceased to be an 'error' and became authentic. These drawings are the witnesses. Art can cross boundaries, assimilate the contradiction between representation and imagination – but succeeds only if it is made with intent.

⌒ Think of two or three abstract artists you admire, artists whose subjects are chosen from the visible world and who change or abstract them in various ways. Consider their work in terms of the choice to involve the imagination, to cross perceptual boundaries.

Disturbing images

These off-scale drawings, especially of the female model, are also deeply disturbing: the big, heavy body with the tiny pods or paws represents helplessness and impotence. Hands are the instruments of doing and changing; you get out there and *manhandle* the world. Feet are the weight-bearers and movers – you stand upright on them, move confidently from place to place. But these drawings are images of apathy and weakness – how could anyone touch or embrace with such fragile hands? Walk, or even crawl, with such crippled feet? We recognize and are moved by this creative depiction of incapacity.

These drawings also recall ancient Maltese fertility statues or the best of Inuit carvings. But it is not just that they remind us of time-hallowed primitive art. They stand with them, attuned to that same 'primitive' source – the truth of the invariant representation.

The other exaggeration

Drawing hands and feet too small on purpose takes courage. So does the other exaggeration.

⌒ Make one drawing labelled VERY BIG HANDS AND FEET. Draw in the same way, but exaggeratedly enlarge the hands and feet.

If you are cautious, the difference between your first drawings and this one will be minimal. In fact, your VERY BIG HANDS AND FEET may turn out to be almost the correct size, verging perhaps a little on the small side. Being cautious means depending without realizing it on the invariant image. At the same time, it was caution that prevented your making them extra small in the first exercise.

Drawings with grossly oversized feet and hands are novelties indeed, and set up all sorts of discords and excitement in the observer. Perhaps they are tuning in to the homunculus with its humungous thumb. New drawings, new searchings, are always a pleasure to look at – and in that sense beautiful.

Back to ripeness of sight

You have been isolating and object-making with a vengeance. It is time now to return to your new, open vision, to bring the hands and feet back, through a series of drawings, into their real place in the world.

Look at how your hand or foot, or the model's, extends from arm or leg. Choose interesting, unusual (difficult) poses.

First, make a drawing of the shape of space touching hand or foot, moving in like bays between promontories. Be sure you include the space touching wrist or ankle as well.

As you found, named and drew torm and *lumb*, do the same for how hands and feet extend through wrists and ankles. Call these areas hand- and *foot-roots*.

⌒◯ *Draw, using long grey lines or smudges of direction,*
then making the contours from the arm out into the hand,
or from the leg out into the foot. See how the form widens.
Draw at least life-sized. Don't 'finish off'.

Remember making 'blind' drawings while not looking down at the paper?

⌒◯ *Make some quick blind drawings now, of your hand*
or foot in different poses. The fingers will look like
bananas but for once they will be big enough.

There is a nameless, almost always overlooked direction in the hand – the interosseus muscle between thumb and forefinger. This is seldom given enough space. If you held your hand out prone, with fingers touching, and checked the line of the inner wrist, where would it go? Most people believe it would bisect thumb and forefinger, i.e. only the thumb would stick from of it.

⌒◯ *Try this. As you now can see, such an*
imaginary line would carry through the hand and
along the inner side of the forefinger as well. What
happens between thumb and forefinger is way outside
this line, and goes off in another direction entirely.
Can you see it?
    Make a drawing of the prone hand, and trace this
new, nameless direction. Add an arrow outside the
form to continue it off into space. Maybe we should
find it a name – we will call it the thangle. *Try*
finding and drawing it in other hand gestures. Look

for the thangle *whenever you draw hands – nameless, it was hardly ever noticed; now, seeing it and saying its name, and recording its truth, will make your drawings of hands beautiful.*

The hand has a secret lanuage.

Try some graceful wrist movements. Draw each one in the same way, beginning with marks of direction, ending with contours along the wrist, and at the beginning of the thumb and fingers. Again, don't 'finish off'.

Rodin made numerous studies of a troupe of Cambodian dancers who had come to France. He was bewitched in particular by their hand movements. 'I followed them to Marseilles. I would follow them to Africa. When they left I thought they had taken away the beauty of the world.'

The gesture of the wrist is the secret language of the hand – if you have heard it your problems with drawing hands will be over. Try to listen.

The riddle of truth

The *thangle* is an instance of the riddle of truth – anyone, looking at the drawing which records it, will accept it immediately as true and find it beautiful. How can a nameless, unacknowledged, literally unknown truth be recognized? Does the hand-invariant know about it after all? Is it secretly stored as memory, and if so, where? Is there a hidden compartment in the back of the drawer? Why can't we get at it when we visualize the hand-invariant; why are we so persistently expected (by the brain) to draw hands without it? If it is stored, why this shock of pleasure?

The torso

Another area of the body where the Perky effect prevails is the torso, in particular, the breasts and spine. It would be superfluous to make a drawing exercise out of exaggerating them.

If you look at the torso from the back you can possibly make out, down the middle, the two long erector spinae muscles. They are at rest if the model is standing erect; only in the act of straightening up or bending over do they come into play. Between them the knobby vertebrae lie in their long groove. On the front of the torso you see, definitely, two round breasts with some shadows under, on, and around them. If the model is male, you still see the nipples.

As markers

Breasts and spine tend to be used as markers – whatever the pose, you locate them early on as points of reference. If you have drawn from life you will agree there's a kind of satisfaction ('Now I know where I am') in pinpointing the nipples or placing the spine line. In keeping with the Perky effect, this marking of named, significant objects actually makes them less visible; the brain has now come through with its top-down invariant, and it isn't necessary to look any more. You have a feeling of 'problem solved' – now you can get on with the drawing.

Breasts and spine are so significant in themselves that it's natural to isolate and accentuate them. If you imagine a torso, these invariants will appear as the most important subsets on it.

Worst case scenario

If you wander around a life drawing class, you'll see, first, that there's little or no attention paid to the basic form of the torso. It has been broken up by deep modelling, its wholeness neglected in favour of chosen particulars; the spine, the breasts. Second, these particulars are not accurately drawn. In academic life drawings, the spine predictably appears as a line, and that line has hardly anything to do with the pose; the middle of the model's back may have had a couple of blurry shadows on it, a change of tone far weaker than that along the side of the figure – or nothing at all.

As for the breasts, they are happily homed in on, while their relationship to the rest of the torso is left out. Any 'shading' or 'modelling' carves deeply around them. In a worst case scenario they sport blackened aureoles that read like bullet holes in the surface.

The nose

Again, it is worth mentioning the nose. Drawing lines or vertical shadows down either side of the elevation we call *nose* is similar to gouging out the spine. The brain likes clear boundaries around objects, and according to the brain the nose is an object and it wants you to put lines around it, and spherical black nostrils on it, and you end up with something like the cut-out on a cornflakes box.

It is extraordinary how entrenched the idea of 'spine', and of vertical, isolated 'nose', can be. People will argue fiercely for the right to draw them in, even when their visible existence is but a faint breath on the model, or none at all. Part of this is a constancy issue (remember how you tried to perceive the mysteriously changing value of tone against background?).

But their significance also marks them. A far darker tone, say the shadow under the shoulder blade or buttocks, or (on the face) the shadow under the chin, goes unseen because it is nameless and, therefore, without importance. Lines and emphatic gouging proclaim the invariant representation, and in each case disrupt the whole form on which these minor surface variations may or may not be visible.

Drawing by exclusion

What would it be like to draw without the safety-net of significant objects? To choose to exclude them, giving up your usual procedure of using them as markers?

Make a drawing of the torso omitting the spine and/or breasts. If you don't have access to a model, make two drawings from imagination.

You may be confused, even indignant. You may be asking, 'What am I supposed to do – just leave them out? What then am I supposed to draw?' In this case any attempted drawing is a witness that, for you, there wasn't much else to draw, certainly nothing of interest. You might have drawn the breasts anyway – you 'couldn't help it' or didn't take the directions seriously. Now is the time to proceed in a more positive way – to begin to discover what else there is to see.

Once I taught a Danish night school class with a young, blonde model who was rather stiff and shy. She had very large breasts which were certainly her most interesting aspect. Week after week, people enjoyed themselves drawing big, bulging breasts, and nothing much else was happening. Finally in exasperation I wrote on the blackboard:

BRYSTFORBUD (breasts prohibited). The students were quite reasonably upset. The first reaction was of course negative. Why eliminate what were so unquestionably, delightfully there? And by forbidding them, was I not in fact bringing them to everyone's attention even more? In spite of these concerns, the drawings improved dramatically.

Freeing yourself to see

First of all, the Perky effect made it doubtful anyone was drawing the breasts accurately anyway. Secondly, nobody was seeing much of anything else. *Brystforbud* meant, and still means, freeing the attention. No longer fixated on the super-significant objects, no longer inundated by a flood of top-down generalization, you are at liberty to see what else is there. And this freedom applies to all aspects of drawing – it's a matter of making new, deliberate choices. Choosing to exclude a very loaded object is a good start. Choosing something else to lavish your attention on is suddenly possible, even easy. This is the freedom Iris Murdoch called the *freedom from fantasy*.

If you don't have access to a model, use your own torso in a mirror. Write on the top of the paper NO BREASTS (or NO PECTORALS). Draw again.

At this point, you might become worried about how much you ought to draw, and where exactly you should stop. Great. When you begin answering this question for yourself, as you draw, you'll realize there is no exact division. When you stop object-making you begin to see.

Drawing the torso in this way frees you to discover

everything you never heeded before. I won't try here to make a list of what is before you, only say that you will be going out into unexplored territory filled with surprises and delights. Above all, you'll come to understand that the torso is a unified form, a central pillar from which the rest of the body extends.

No spine line from now on

In future, don't bother drawing the spine. Whenever you're drawing the back and your attention is caught by a central shadow, and you are tempted, stop for a moment. Squint your eyes until it blurs into the whole, and note how unimportant it really is. Surely it is better to leave it out entirely. Because you are almost bound to say too much. (If you do not believe this is true, try it.)

Breasts as part of the whole

As for the breasts, you have realized by now they are not balloons to be casually stuck on. The place where your attention is required is a nameless *how* – how they merge into the rest. Copying cast shadows, or any emphatic darkening of the surface, which the eye is bound to read as deep incursions, destroys the unity of the torso and forces areas away which are actually close. This goes for any form – a knee, the face. Superficial detail nearest you needs to be almost breathless, left to bask in the proximate, pale light of your observation.

Fetish and erotic drawing

Colouring in the aureoles or outlining them disturbs the form. They look like fried eggs. You are modelling the surface, not making a cartoon. In a modelled drawing, superficial tonal differences create spatial disharmony. And of course there is no visible line around them, only what a painter might want to remark – a slight change of colour and possibly tone.

The same kind of outlining and shading can show up with what we call the *lips*. Lips and aureoles are among the brain's choice invariants – important, isolated objects, in this case loaded with sexual significance. There is no line around the lips, only around the idea of them. Drawing them within a bounding line and colouring them dark is the brain's idea. You are responding to an erotically encumbered image.

It is the same as with hands and feet: when these areas are isolated as *objects*, they become carriers of huge cargos of meaning. The artist can take responsibility, and use them to effect. Egon Schiele knew well what he was doing in his images of the tense, erotically charged body. In his drawings, even the fingernails simmer with sexual tension. As do David Hockney's otherwise restrained line portraits of boys when he chooses to download the sensuality of the lips by drawing lines around them.

Lips, like breasts, are powerful images, and if they are allowed to impose unconsciously they make for 'bad' (boring and predictable) art. It would be interesting to try excluding them as well, and see what happens.

The mouth muscle

It is possible, with a bit of a struggle, to describe the mouth muscle without even referring to the lips. As follows:

The *orbicularis ori* or mouth muscle is a big, tough, mobile, fibrous sphincter. It looks a bit like a pancake with a centre slit, slapped over the lower front of the face. It is inserted into the skin. It covers the face area from under the nose, down the inside of the cheek furrows, and – pouched and buttoned – across the middle of the chin.

Use a mirror or model, and choose to see the whole mouth muscle rather than the lips. You can see its boundaries if you look for them. Ignore the idea of lips entirely. You can, of course, draw the slit. Make several drawings, using different angles and lighting.

If you study master drawings you won't see lips. Check out Holbein to understand how little is necessary, if that little is true.

Cartoons

Cartoons make deliberate use of the invariant. They are the ultimate distillation – round balloon breasts, a big nose, a sharp line around the lips, are 'funny' signals everyone recognizes. (The reason we did not bother with a gestalt exercise to exaggerate breasts and spine is that we would have been making cartoons.) Gary Larson's wonderful animals tingle with life, largely because of the audacious, nervy line along their spines. Like caricaturists, cartoonists teach us their style, what they each choose to isolate and exaggerate. A new cartoonist takes a while to get used to, just as attempted caricatures of the newly famous take a while to fix on some characteristic, and the public comes to award it with recognition. The early caricatures of Jimmy Carter, for example, did not fix on his teeth, and Reagan's even features resisted caricaturizing for some time, before his jaw became the accepted focus. It has been a study to see how caricatures of George W. Bush moved gradually through stages into his simian likeness.

Face once more

The face flattens and stands forward in many figure drawings, tending to be treated differently from the rest of the figure. Remember how much courage it took, in the modelled drawings, to press the face back where it belonged? Face is the most powerful image of all. What about making an experimental drawing where Perls' gestalt exaggeration was applied to *face*? What would happen?

The original idea behind this experiment was that the 'error' of the flat, picky face would become obvious, and could thereafter be avoided. Again, result turned out to be different from intent.

Look directly at yourself in the mirror, or at a model. The pose should be formal – the figure staring straight ahead, seated cross-legged or on a chair with hands open loosely on the knees. Make a big, dense drawing, working from the solid form of the hands and thighs right up through the head. The figure need not be solidly black, and it can contain details of contour and modelled form, but it has to be dense, that is, with no air holes or whitish light areas – except for the face. Leave the face blank.

Decide precisely what you mean by 'face' and make explicit boundaries, as if it were a mask. The neck and hair are dark right up to where the face begins. Check to make sure the whole body is densely dark before you continue.

To draw the face, choose a different, more precise tool. Work sequentially and lineally. Just as when you were drawing small hands and feet, this work should be pleasurable – you can indulge yourself, give in to the numinous invariant. Lines around the lips are fine. Darken the lips and the irises if you want. Very slight shading is allowed, too. Put in all the details, to the last eyelash. Soft white chalk or pastel can be used to keep the face white, if it happens to get smudged. What you are aiming for is a discrete face, a kind of mask. When the drawing is finished, put it on the wall.

The secret of the mask

The quality of this figure is hard to describe – it has a look, and that look is inward, cerebral, austere. The deliberate clash between this almost iconicized *face* and the heavy, dark, powerfully sensual body is extraordinarily exciting. Something is ticking in the drawing. From the wall, the figure gazes forward with an obscure authority. What is happening?

Somehow you have tuned in to the most potent symbol of all. This drawn face outstares you – unique, unforgettable, recognized. It joins the host of images artists have made throughout history, and go on making, in their desire to understand and celebrate humanity.

The white face on a figure whose form – usually breasts or hands – still contains some 'air holes' or near-white bits, will not work. The figure needs to be completely dense. Otherwise the observer's gaze jumps from the face down to those light patches.

If your drawing still has light bits for the eye to jump to, darken them carefully and thoroughly so not a chink is left to compete with the white face. Now see the difference.

Now, looking at the whole figure, your eyes are not diverted but rest absolutely on the face, and find there a strong presence, intelligence and dignity.

Oddly, the face on its own would not carry the same punch as in its relation to the dark figure. (Try covering the rest of the figure to confirm this.) The secret seems to be in the juxtaposition, here presented graphically and at its most extreme, between the body and the mind. One plays off the other. The drawing tunes into a fundamental, universal human experience. The mind is housed in and dependent on the body, yet it keeps itself apart. This is a drawing of the mysterious, embodied mind.

The face in life drawing

Artists making life drawings usually have the sense to ignore, even blacken out, the face. They know its ultimate unimportance to the wholeness of the form, where even the head, as Rodin would say, is not a separate part, but 'everywhere'. The following exercise is optional.

 Blacken the face.

This might be too difficult, and obviously it's your choice. Your drawing might be one you would not consider defacing. Even the word *deface* has a strong negative connotation: to deface means to impair and disfigure, as well as just to obliterate. Closer is the word *efface*, which means not only to obliterate but also 'to cause to be unnoticed, inconspicuous'. The act of wiping out the features is daring – flagrant, even – if you had to wipe out a hand or a buttock you wouldn't be nearly so upset. The invariant holds you like a vice. Instead, you might prefer to play with effacing other figure drawings – those in which the face-invariant pushed in rather than was summoned – and seeing how they change for the better.

The warp of truth

Through this work you have learned that the inner image – the invariant – can be not only generalized or idealized, but also warped, and how distortion makes for mediocre art if it is allowed to sneak into your work.

You have also learned that a warp can also be a truth – the truth of our consensual imagination. And that it has great power, if you pay attention to it and incorporate it consciously into your art.

We have used the example of the human body. The lesson applies to any objects an artist may encounter and choose to work with, because they are all determined as objects by the brain, and all are invariants.

Think of other objects for a work of art. Or think of abstract paintings you have seen. An example would be a Braque still life. Ask yourself – how is the artist tapping into, and celebrating, the invariant? Is it conscious and intelligent? Can you imagine an object you want to work with, or are working with, in these terms?

The Sources of Creativity

One has to be poor unto the tenth generation... to feel beyond them into the roots and into the earth itself. One has to be able at every moment to place one's hand on the earth like the first human being.

Rainer Maria Rilke

Y ou have been exploring perception and creation, the act of sight and the act of making, and have run up against riddles which appear unsolvable. It is time to bring the various threads together. The big question is whether you, as an artist, can access the world? A world which is unfamiliar, nameless, perhaps unknowable?

If there is a gate, where is it and how can you find your way? This is not just an academic question. It involves you and your creativity.

The role of attention

Like a dragon sitting on its hoard of treasure, the greedy brain guards its invariants, and continues to categorize and compensate, recognize, and even predict, how we are to see. As artists, maybe we do not have to accept, passively, what the brain decides. We can continue to look and nurture our sight, choosing consciously, prepared to be in touch with the unexpected, the surprising, the new. Attention is the key.

Attention is a state of expectancy, a readiness to respond at the threshold of responding, a 'volume control on an amplifier' which directly affects neuron activity. Visual attention and eye movement systems share the same areas of the brain, and use the same mechanisms. It is attention that sends new information upward on the visual pathway, assembling new patterns higher and higher. Attention has been called the *glue* which binds shape and colour together, even though (this is the *binding problem*) they are processed in different consciousnesses, different parts of the brain.

The idea of synchrony

Cells interchange bits of chemicals directly through the synapses between them. Another circuitry is independent of physical synapses – the electrical one. Cells send electrical impulses across chasms and abysses, allowing other cells, and whole networks, to fire in a coordinated way.

When you are paying attention, there are measurable changes in EEG (electro-encephalogram) activity. These various waves can be charted and watched on a screen as they cross the brain. We all know the cliché for death in hospital films – all the lines go flat.

When you are awake but unfocused, the alpha waves predominate. In the *attentional state*, there is a beta-burst in the thalamic cells, which causes *gamma waves* to take over. Electrical impulses can leap across spaces of millimetres – and during attention, synchronized oscillations build up which can regroup whole areas into large-scale networks. The idea is that these waves, brought into synchrony by attention, unite the brain, thus solving the riddle of separate consciousnesses – separate modules for different attributes – the *binding problem*.

Memory and the new

For simplicity's sake we have imagined a direct highway from the eyes to the higher cortical areas of the brain. Actually the system is far more complex, with the equivalent of toll gates and stopovers, detours and diversions, loops, roundabouts, traffic islands and shopping centres, and – according to the most persuasive story – two-way traffic with abrupt U-turns and lane changes as well.

One station is the *thalamus*. It is the relay point for all sensory information except smell, and is essential for processing information to be stored as memory. It also directs attention – an attribute vital to creativity.

It is thought that the thalamus regulates the brain's electrical rhythms, so the parts of the brain can communicate with other parts in gamma wave synchrony. A 'fleeting memory', likened to a spotlight across a stage, swings across the brain. The brain is said to 'raise a chorus' as attention increases. Alternatively, when the rhythms don't quite synchronize, you get that frustrating tip-of-the-tongue experience – more recently called a 'senior moment' – when you're trying to remember a name or bit of information you know perfectly well but can't quite access.

Some cells inhibit or close down activity in other cells. Most of the time, the inhibitory cells in the thalamus are hanging out and not doing anything much, but when the brain gets over-excited they can act like a kind of pacemaker, or the governor on an engine, and keep it from running away into seizure. The dangerous, accelerating pulse of synchrony is slowed down and brought to a halt. It is important that the brain has this ability to desynchronize.

New assemblies

Another station is the *hippocampus* (so named because of its sea-horse shape). A direct pathway links it to the sensory cortex. It's the centre for navigation and short-cuts – London taxi drivers, who must possess 'The Knowledge,' are found to have enlarged posterior hippocampi. Here a spatial representation of the entire city of London is claimed to be stored, which the hippocampus has expanded to accommodate.

The relationship of the hippocampus to memory is thought to be crucial. It stores personal or episodic memory, especially as connected to our emotions, and consolidates lasting memory for transfer to other areas. For us as artists, its most interesting attribute is that it receives new assemblies which have reached it unhindered, climbing up and up the hierarchy in search of something recognizable to engage and pattern with.

The ascent of the *torm*

Here's an example. If we go back to how we named and identified 'new' areas of the human body, we find the torm. Let us choose to follow its initial ascent towards memory. There is not much in its way (though a pattern for 'shoulder' may come shouldering down and try to reshape it) and the patterns causing it to cohere as an object are new. You drew the torm several times; repetition strengthened the synapses, and eventually you 'committed it to memory'. Now, if you conjure up an image of the torm, it will appear, retrieved out of the store. In your visual cortex, neurons devoted to its contours will blink and respond – perhaps a little sleepily, but respond nevertheless.

Been there, done that

Oddly, there is a *decrease* in cell activity when we encounter something new. If what we see is familiar – something related to our past – its invariant pattern is already in place and the signal is casual and rapid. It's a neural shrug of complacency – *been there, done that*.

With new information – the unfamiliar – the process is more complex: at eye level a great many dull, broadly tuned neurons sock in, none of which is capable of saying much of interest. Then the overall number decreases markedly – all these drowsier cells are suppressed and their task taken over by fewer, sharper, more discriminating ones. It's called the *grocery cart problem* – we throw in only the significant and leave piles of irrelevant information behind on the shelves. The work of processing up the visual pathway has begun.

Take our example of the torm, and how we first saw it: this truly novel assembly shimmers and coheres within its contours as it escalates, further and further up the pathway. The longer it goes without being recognized and interrupted, and the more often the same pattern, seen again, comes swarming up in its wake, the better chance it has of reaching memory. Finally this new, consolidated entity is learned – encoded into the store. It can then move down and meet the next *torm* we see, as an invariant representation.

Natural and unnatural colour

The Fauvists were the first painters to 'liberate' colour,

deliberately applying unnatural colours to objects to evoke a strong emotional response. Because shape and its colour is experienced as absolutely, inextricably bound, looking at a Fauvist painting (say a blue horse) is a shock. What is happening in the brain?

Zeki describes how natural colour activates V4 (the colour centre), and an area in front of it. Cells in the hippocampus are also excited and, over in the right hemisphere, cells in the lower part of the frontal lobe.

But what happens when you look at a blue horse? Apparently the unnatural colour, while still activating V4, skips the hippocampus entirely, and in the frontal lobe a completely different, central area leaps to life. This area has been called a *monitoring station* – and it responds to the unusual, the new.

The frontal lobes

Frontal lobes are, as you would expect, at the front. Eastern philosophy was dead-on in locating the third eye in the forehead, because the region of the brain behind it is definitely the most important to us as humans. The frontal lobes have been called the 'organ of civilization' – everything we really care about is mediated here. Herein lies our intelligence, judgement and decision-making, attention and emotion, recognition and – for our purposes most important of all – our ability to take in new information. The frontal lobes are a kind of slate on which, moment by moment, is scrawled the ongoing script of our lives. The unfamiliar gains its access here in the central *monitoring station* and, as if written in water, briefly appears before it is appropriated and sent on. Here for a short time the utterly strange is held up and separately distinguished from the ordinary. And here is your selective attention, prepared to see it.

Conflict and resolution

Here, incoming information is monitored for any conflict with the habitual, predictable view, monitored for anything that needs resolving to bring it into line. I find the terms 'conflict' and 'needs resolving' negatively loaded. Surely here, in the monitoring station, is our chance as artists to embrace the conflict and stave off the resolution, to touch and choose what is new and as yet untampered with – the very raw stuff of the world.

Access to creativity

The 'mad artist' is a kind of cartoon character in our culture, but the general idea – that the artist is slightly (or more than slightly) unhinged – prevails, and it has its sources. Creativity is, after all, the ability to make uncommon, unique connections. I've underlined how necessary it is for the artist to be open, to have the courage to make choices – including unusual and risky ones. Now it appears there is a definite functional, even biological similarity between the brains of creative people and mentally unstable ones.

Normal people have good, efficient inhibitions. They are naturally cautious and conventional, and get along in life well within the bounds of their predictions and expectations, comfortably screening out anything risky or new. Their inhibitory system works well for them. They are said to have good *latent inhibition*.

Slightly odd people – those who might be termed 'schizotypes' or 'borderline', share with artists a measurably low level of *latent inhibition*. For this reason, they are open to the unfamiliar in the world. This makes them vulnerable. The artist, while sharing the vulnerability, has the gift of creative intelligence. Faced with the potentially dangerous onslaught of the new, the artist is not its prey, but its welcoming host. The artist is protected by being able to choose, edit, discriminate, spark off connections, work the system.

Creative people have been shown to be more likely to use their brains bilaterally. They have more access to, and freer communication between, the hemispheres. Studies of the brains of boys who are highly gifted in mathematics, music or art show that they are organized quite differently from normal brains, and the functions usually hoarded by one hemisphere appear globally. The creative mind has special, open access, and this means more flow and cooperation between the verbal and the spatial intelligences. The artist has the ability to mix established patterns and make unique new ones, to play seriously, and to work playfully.

The apprentice

It's useful to look back at the place of art in the past; what daily life must have been like for artists in other cultures and at other times.

Imagine being transported back to ancient Egypt, about two thousand years BC. *You are young and talented and 'want to be an artist'. How would you go about it? What would have been important to you then, and what would be your goal? What steps would you need to take?*

Now imagine yourself in fourteenth-century Italy, and ask the same questions.

It's obvious that, almost universally, art was anonymous. Artists functioned in the mainstream, working for the rulers who in turn supported them. The purpose of art in Egypt was preservation of the pharaohs, the ensuring of their continuance in a spiritual kingdom that embraced the earthly one as well – past, present and future. Even the concept of 'wanting to be an artist' would not have been understood; your goal would have been better voiced as 'wanting to be a craftsman'. Artists as masters of their craft were useful and necessary, their place in society secure and unquestioned.

During the Renaissance, even as artists achieved individual fame, much of this still held true – artists were necessary, their skill was highly prized, and they served the demands of the ruling class. Now, however, they had less security and anonymity – they were individuals, subject to the whims of powerful patrons, in a volatile society.

Your primary aim in either society would have been the same, however: to be apprenticed, to learn your craft.

Things are different nowadays. Public art has its place, and grants have replaced patrons – though at an earlier stage in artists' careers, and as a means of support which before would have been supplied by the master. Professional, grown-up artists are usually left to fend for themselves. Nowadays most artists work individually, and want to.

In place of a workshop apprenticeship (and probable continuing employment) there are art schools and degree courses. To apply, you have to prepare a 'portfolio' which shows you have skills and direction already – even some kind of individuality. The emphasis is on you as a person, your 'creativity'. And in our culture 'creativity' is very much an individual, personal attribute. It is equated with being different from others, and being different is often equated with being provocative.

It's true that creative people are different – but to be required to be so (especially early on) and to strive to be so is a funny way to go about it. In a way, the present necessity of being different has made everyone the same. It is very rare indeed that something really new happens in art, and the reason is that art builds on art and is immersed inthe culture. You learn from other artists through a long apprenticeship, whether it is in a workshop or not. Modern apprenticeship tends to be piecemeal. On the other hand, the culture is inundated with images, as never before. We can choose images from any age and in any style, and it may look as though there are no rules any more. There are; we are stuck in the culture and can't see objectively, just as the Egyptian stonemason and the Renaissance painter were stuck in theirs. True creativity is not superficial and does not consist of striving to be different or provocative. Its sources lie deeper than the personal, and access is not easy.

The poverty of the gift

The Gift by Lewis Hyde, is a wise book about working creatively within a money-based society. He writes that as artists we must strive to remain somehow in a state of 'interior poverty'. It is as if our gifts are not fully ours 'until they are given away'. Hyde quotes from Leviticus: The Lord said to Moses, *The land shall not be sold in perpetuity, for the land is mine; for you are strangers and sojourners with me.*

Creative energy

It's said that we each have a certain supply of energy to use from day to day and throughout our lives. Where is your creative energy directed? Wherever it goes means less energy available for somewhere else. If your creative energy is spent on the effort to be different, you are using it, and depleting it, on a superficial level. Real creativity creates its own differences. Your task is somehow to find this source, and get out of the way.

'Art ought not to show itself off', wrote Pasternak, but be, 'sunk in obscurity, in the back rows, hardly aware that its hat is aflame on its head'.

The proper human goal

'It is a *task* to come to see the world as it is,' wrote Iris Murdoch. Art is 'an excellent analogy of morals, or indeed… a case of morals'. In mediocre art, even more clearly than in mediocre conduct, you see 'the intrusion of fantasy, the assertion of self, the dimming of any reflection of the real world'. Have we come any closer to understanding what she called *fantasy* and what she called *real?*

Is freedom from fantasy a proper human goal? Is it a proper goal for the artist? Fantasy is superficial and keeps us superficially stuck at the level of the ego. Imagination will remain impoverished unless we seek to nourish and enrich it through our senses, by open, selfless attention to the radiance of the world.

Difficulty

Our task is not easy, perhaps not even possible. Think of Cézanne, whom Rilke described as 'sitting in this garden, like an old dog. The dog of his work which he calls to him again and again and beats him and lets him go hungry. And yet with it all, the dog clings to this incomprehensible master'. Giacometti drew his subjects over and over, hundreds of times. He said, 'It might be that, if I could hold you there before me for many years, even more, perhaps I could then, certainly not completely, succeed in cancelling that margin of imperfection that always remains in my attempts to truly know who and what you are.'

We do not attain truth, yet truth is there in the striving for it. The psychiatrist R. D. Laing expressed the riddle in these words: 'The truth I am trying to grasp is the me that is trying to grasp it.'

When it is difficult enough, and interesting enough, your attention will settle in and you will understand what Giacometti meant when he said he worked 'only for the sensation that is mine when I work'. This brings us full circle. Rilke said that the emotion that brings you to the work should be 'so thoroughly exhausted in the act of making, there is no residue'.

Fantasy or imagination?

> '*Thou art in Error, trouble me not with thy righteousness.*
> '*I have innocence to defend and ignorance to instruct!*'
>
> William Blake

You have experienced how the invariant representation in the brain seems to be trying continuously to wrest the attention away from the senses. This is no polite debate between two intellectual modes, but occurs volcanically, profoundly shaping and recharging the very structures of perception. We know at first hand its power and numinosity, and its central importance in our creative life.

This is the arena. Here creativity stands, saying: 'I have innocence to defend and ignorance to instruct.'

For William Blake, the visual system was a blacksmith's forge, where 'innocent' sensory perception struck alternately with the 'ignorant' but instructed mind. In his prophetic book *Jerusalem* he commands:

> 'Take thou this Hammer & in patience heave the
> thundering Bellows;
> 'Take thou these Tongs; strike thou alternate with me,
> labour obedient.'

The 'big area of fantasy activity', which Perls called No Man's Land, 'takes up all the energy, all the excitement, so that very little is free to be in touch with yourself or the world'. Not fantasy but imagination is the central concept of Blake's cosmology; it is his authentic reality. In the imagination of his genius, he was able to move at will into regions that are even now, at most, only timidly and superficially charted by psychiatry. He had the genius to comprehend the creative imagination as a vigorous, organic reality, not opposed to or objectively different from the world but bound inalienably into it through the continuous work of perception. What was unreal to Blake was the abstract folly, or fantasy. In a letter, he described his ongoing battle:

'I labour incessantly & accomplish not one half of what I intend, because Abstract folly hurries me often away while I am at work, carrying me over Mountains and Valleys, which are not Real, in a land of Abstraction where Spectres of the dead wander. This I endeavour to prevent and with my whole might chain my feet to the world of Duty and Reality; but in vain! the faster I bind, the better is the Ballast.'

Instructing ignorance

Uninstructed, the invariants may continue to contaminate your work, keeping it at the level of the expected, generalized and predictable. Unconfronted, they will continue to be saboteurs in your search for truth, pulling you back into the intermediate zone of fantasy. If they are to work for you, they must first be engaged in the arena at a conscious level, and 'strike alternate' with your open, 'innocent' attention to the world. To make conscious is an act of befriending – they will change in the light. If you work honestly you cannot help being 'imaginative' in this best sense of the word, in touch with the radiance of consciousness and with the radiance of the world.

Explaining the sources

This book has sought to explain the sources of visual creativity. It is exciting and instructive to learn more about what we, as artists, are up to, and why. To explore how we see, imagine, attend and remember.

What was the wordless property of the artist is now being explored, charted and systematized on this last frontier of human knowledge. As yet, disagreements and contradictions accompany the excitement of detection and discovery on all levels. 'After 50 years of work,' wrote Beau Lotto and Dale Purves in 2000, 'neurobiologists still can't explain in terms of visual circuitry any aspect of visual perception, no matter how simple.' Much has happened since, not least in their own field; much is still unknown.

My purpose has been to present and celebrate what makes sense in terms of my own experience as an artist and teacher. I believe that the more we know the answers to the questions of *how* and *why*, the more creative we can be.

We learn as well from fragments of wisdom the artists themselves impart – and strangely enough it's often the words of artists, poets and mystics which illuminate the 'facts', not the other way around. But there's no polarity really, or even a confrontation. For example, poet Christopher Dewdney and neurobiologist Semir Zeki move effortlessly across the boundary between poetry and science and make us realize that the boundary, like the bands of the rainbow, is not really there.

Look up from this book, and see what is before you.

You began in this room with the book in your hands, doing a simple visual exercise. Here is where you end as well, with Kafka's famous words for a conclusion:

> *You do not need to leave your room. Remain sitting at your table and listen. Do not even listen, simply wait, be quiet, still and solitary. The world will freely offer itself to you to be unmasked, it has no choice, it will roll in ecstasy at your feet.*

Workshops with Heather Spears

Heather Spears has developed her unique teaching method over decades of workshop instruction in Europe and America. In this book, she gathers her experiences into a manual for working artists, for use in the studio and at home.

Her workshops comprise ordinary drawing classes of about 15 students. They run for up to five days, and are highly structured (people are challenged to take risks, and expected to follow instructions). Heather teaches by presenting an exercise verbally. Students note the instructions on their paper, and resulting criticism/discussion comes from everyone looking at the results. During rests Heather discusses perception in the light of new findings about the visual brain, and uses many examples of master drawings and from literature.

Intensive life drawing classes

This course follows the exercises in the book most closely. A model is present for all sessions.

Drawing the figure in motion

In this two-day course, the students begin in a classroom, then draw on location (usually a sports hall or music/dance rehearsal), meeting at intervals to discuss their work. Here, because of the difficulty, students are asked to make a contract not to give up. Often the sketches result in an impromptu exhibition.

Heather also teaches two separate courses on the human head:

1 Modelling the human head in clay: Heather uses human craniums as models, with three or four students working from each and building it accurately in clay. Muscles, and finally the features, are progressively added to the clay skull, while the action is discussed and demonstrated. Growth, likeness, expression and recognition are ongoing themes. Students who have never drawn are able to make a stunningly realistic head in this way, and its value for drawing and painting portraits can't be overestimated.

The course includes instruction in finishing and firing the heads.

2 Drawing the human head: As emphasized in this book, head rather than face is what matters in portraying age, likeness and even expression. This workshop begins by concentrating on the structure of the head, and ends with stance (how the head sits on the shoulders). This is a lively workshop with many different models – from the newborn baby through children of different ages, to the very old, as well as models of differing ethnicity. Students study master portraits and the work of other cultures, and use colour and various media as well.

Heather continues to explore and write about visual perception, and invites readers' participation. Please join in and respond to more new experiments in seeing and creating by going to: **www.heatherspears.com/visionexperiments** for details.

Acknowledgements

With thanks to Dr. Jack Cohen for his generous advice on the scientific parts of the text.

p.6 Excerpt from 'Markings' from *Seeing Things* by Seamus Heaney, Faber and Faber Ltd 1991; p.14 'The teaching of drawing (a line is)' from 'The Word for Sand' 1986 from *Poems: Selected and New* by Heather Spears. Reprinted by permission of Heather Spears and Wolsak and Wynn Publishers Ltd; p.15 Excerpt from *Mystical Poems* 1968 by Jalal al-Din Rumi, (tr. A. J. Arberry). Published by, and copyright © University of Chicago Press; p.17 Excerpt from 'Paravisual flooding' from *The Immaculate Perception* by Christopher Dewdney, House of Anansi, Toronto 1986. Reprinted by permission of the publishers and Christopher Dewdney; p.19-20 Excerpts from 'Epilogue', 'Fishnet' and 'The Flaw' from *Collected Poems* by Robert Lowell. Copyright © 2003 by Harriet Lowell and Sheridan Lowell. Reprinted by permission of Farrar, Straus and Giroux, LLC; p.23 'The City Limits'. Copyright ©1971 by A. R. Ammons, from *The Selected Poems, Expanded Edition* by A. R. Ammons. Used by permission of W.W. Norton & Company, Inc; p.24 Excerpt from 'The Sidewalk' by Margaret Atwood. Originally published in *Interlunar* ©1984 by Margeret Atwood. Reprinted by permission of the author; p.28 'Hydrocephalus obs.' from 'How Animals See', from *Poems: Selected and New* by Heather Spears. Reprinted by permission of Heather Spears and Wolsak and Wynn Publishers Ltd; p.63 Extract from 'The Man with the Blue Guitar' from *The Collected Poems of Wallace Stevens* by Wallace Stevens, ©1954 by Wallace Stevens and renewed 1982 by Holly Stevens. Used by permission of Alfred A. Knopf, a division of Random House, Inc; Michelangelo print on frontispiece, *Studies for the Libyan Sibyl*: The Metropolitan Museum of Art, Purchase, Joseph Pulitzer Bequest, 1924 (24.197.2r). Image © The Metropolitan Museum of Art

Bibliography

Wade, Nicholas and Swanston, Michael *Visual Perception* (Routledge, 1991)

Harth, Erich *Windows of the Mind* (William Morrow and Co, 1981)

Nicolaides, Kimon *The Natural Way to Draw* (Houghton Mifflin College Division, 1975)

Irwin, Eleanor *Color Terms in Greek Poetry* (Hakkert, Toronto, 1974)

Berlin, Brent and Kay, Paul *Basic Color Terms* (University of California Press, 1969)

Recommended reading

Dewdney, Christopher. *The Immaculate Perception*. Toronto, House of Anansi Press, 1986.

Hawkins, Jeff. *On Intelligence*. New York, Owl Books, 2005. One of many new, speculative books about the brain, predication and intent.

Hyde, Lewis. *The Gift: Imagination and the Erotic Life of Property*. New York, Vintage Books, 1983. About staying true to your gift while living in a materialistic society.

Lord, James. *A Giacometti Portrait*. New York, Farrar, Strauss and Giroux, 1980.

Rilke, Rainer Maria. *Letters on Cézanne*, transl. Joel Agee, New York, Fromm International, 1988; *Auguste Rodin* transl. Daniel Slager, Brooklyn, Archipelago Books, 2004. This German poet with great insight into visual art wrote movingly on both artists.

Sacks, Oliver. *A Leg to Stand On*, New York, Touchstone Books, 1998 and London, Picador, 1991; *An Anthropologist on Mars*, New York, Vintage Books, 1996 and Picador, London, 1996; *The Island of the Colourblind*, New York, Vintage Books, 1997 and London, Picador, 1997. Wise, celebratory studies of 'abnormal' human conditions.

Zeki, Semir. *Inner Vision, an Exploration of Art and the Brain*. Oxford, Oxford University Press, 1999. A neurobiologist with a profound understanding of art, Zeki shows how art replicates the visual brain's structure and process. This book encouraged me to explore how perception works for and against creativity.

Index